NOTRE DAME IS #1

AND OTHER SPIRITUAL TRUTHS

TIMOTHY L. FORT

TABLE OF CONTENTS

Acknowledgments.............................		2
Dedication.......................................		3
Note to Reader		4
1.	Before There Was Notre Dame......	5
2.	Ground Zero of a Rivalry.............	26
3.	On the Field.............................	44
4:	In the Stands............................	71
5.	Inside the Stadium and Beyond......	95
6.	To Everything There is a Season	120
7.	How God Made Notre Dame #1	130
Index:	....	138
Endnotes:	....	141

ACKNOWLEDGMENTS

While many people can be thanked for their work in the preparation of this book, I would like to single out three:

First, Lisa Cornelio, who edited my meanderings and turned them into something that actually makes sense. She has done this for me so many times that she knows my strengths – always willing to take a whack at a draft – and weaknesses – well, those are a few too many to catalogue.

Second, Tayler Fisher, who provided the artwork for the book is an excellent student of mine at the Kelley School of Business. I later stumbled upon the fact that she was a gifted artist as well. I'm grateful that she agreed to help with the book.

Finally, my daughter Kurina Fort, who checked the index to make sure it was correct and also formatted the document so that it complied with the editorial requirements of CreateSpace.

COPYRIGHT NOTICE

NOTRE DAME IS #1

COPYRIGHT, 2017

TIMOTHY L. FORT

ALL RIGHTS RESERVED

DEDICATION

To all of those who made it possible for me to attend the university of Notre Dame:
Mom, Dad, Kathryn Link, Grandpa Gibb, yes, Ara Parseghian and many others

To those fabulous faculty, students and staff who were with me at Notre Dame:
Including, but not limited to my roommates; Dave, Mace, Shags, Joe, Greg, Dan and John; my singing partners Chad, Terry, Jim, Jeff, Larry, Chris, Pat, Sedge and Jeny

My continued friendships with alumni, faculty, students, and staff at Notre Dame,
which are too numerous to even try to begin to mention

And to all of those who endure (or share) my passion for this remarkable place,
especially my wife Nancy and my children, Kurina, Steven and Theo

NOTE TO READER

It is hard for an academic not to fall into jargon. I have tried avoid it in this book, though I also believe that writing for a Notre Dame audience requires depth. This is hard to do without getting into some arcane material, although I have tried to keep much of the esoteric meanderings in the notes, which appear at the end of the book.

The same holds true, in a different way, for my personal stories. If this book is to be a fan's account of Notre Dame, then I need to tell my own stories as a point of departure. Hearing about me, though, can get really old. Just ask my wife and kids! So I have moved some of those stories to notes as well.

Finally, I have used the same strategies with respect to examples from non-ND sports. We Domers watch more than Notre Dame sports and I want to talk about that in the main body of the book. At the same time, my sense is you are reading this book because you are mainly interested in Notre Dame material. While I will wander beyond the Dome on occasions, I have tried to strike a balance so that I do not do that too much.

CHAPTER ONE

Before There Was Notre Dame: From the Zippers to the Gipper

When the Stronghurst Zippers took the court for the 1967 Illinois State Junior High School Basketball championship, it seemed that all eight hundred people who inhabited the village of Stronghurst stood cheering in the stands. This was big stuff for the little town: the only time one of its school teams had played for the state championship. The windows on the streets of Broadway and Main were adorned with Blue and White signs. The weekly county newspaper was full of Zipper items and the fourteen year old stars of the team were the talk of the Hurry-Back Grill. The rurally-based Zippers had already done the unthinkable: upsetting a team from Chicago. Every resident basked in the reflected glory of the players, who were barely teenagers.

The Zipper fans applauded politely when the heavily-favored team from Pekin Edison ran onto the court. That's the way Stronghurst-ites treated opponents: they cheered hard for their team and a few might have even prayed for their own boys to win, but every player on both sides deserved respect. This also was the state championship game –a moment to savor. Few gave Stronghurst a chance, but the fans believed that if the Zippers competed hard and the fans cheered loudly, they just might pull a huge upset.

One Stronghurst fan, though, started booing the team from Pekin as loudly as he could. The Stronghurst fans tried to shush the nine-year-old trouble-maker, but he was not dissuaded.

Finally, the boy's sister – a cheerleader for the Zippers– came running up into the stands.

"Stop that right now," she said. "Stop booing."

"But I want the Zippers to win."

"So do I, but I am not booing and no else from Stronghurst is either."

"Maybe they should! This is the championship game!"

"Maybe you should grow up and learn to cheer us without booing them."

The boy protested for a few more seconds, but he adored his sister, so he quieted down. He sulked and pouted for most of the first half, but then he started to cheer for the Zippers, who ended up losing the game. He started to understand – just a bit – that he could cheer his team, even when they lost, not be rude and still take in the specialness of the championship game.

I was that nine-year-old boy and this marked the start of lessons on how to be a good fan and how that might make a difference in the way I did other things in life. I could cheer for my side without hating the other side. I could try to succeed in my studies and in the sports I played without needing others to lose for me to win. I could appreciate my team playing in a championship game regardless of whether they won or lost, although I sure preferred they win. In other words, I could embrace the event differently than I had at the start of that game. I was lucky to learn that lesson at the age of nine. Other fans, one might guess from their behavior, must not have had a sister or community to guide them. Or perhaps they didn't listen so well.

For example, on May 25, 1966, soccer fans from Argentina and Peru brawled, leaving 248 dead. Two died and another forty were injured at a game in Bangladesh in 1990.[1] In January, 1991, forty were killed in a South African soccer melee and ten died after a soccer match in Chile five months later.[2] Fourteen people died and 378 were injured in a soccer celebration in Columbia in 1993.[3] Eighty-four people lost their lives in Guatemala and seventy-eight were injured in Zambia in 1996.[4]

In 2006, fans from Germany and England went at it during the World Cup – and Germany was playing Sweden when the fight broke out.[5] Maybe it just the result of an overheated, nationalistic feud. After all, Peru and Argentina and Germany and England have long-standing, national rivalries. But that would be too easy. In 2008, a fight broke out between more than 100 fans in Ohio between a Columbus team and a visiting team from England after fans started to taunt each other.[6] I doubt the War of 1812 was still festering in the fans' minds.

While violence among soccer fans does seem more common than in just about any other sport, that "other football" has produced a few gruesome displays too. In 2007, a 32 year old man walked into a bar in Oklahoma wearing a Texas Longhorn shirt. Words were exchanged and the 53 year old, smaller Sooner supporter (and a church deacon to boot), grabbed the Longhorn's crotch so hard, the younger man's testicles squeezed out. He needed sixty stitches to close the gaping wound.[7]

Neither man attended Texas or Oklahoma, but each one certainly identified with the universities. Remarkably, in a follow-up radio call-in show, Oklahoma fans overwhelmingly agreed that the Longhorn fan had gotten what he deserved.[8]

Welcome to the dark side of sports.

Many times fans identify with their teams is so closely that the "thems" the teams oppose turn quite literally into enemies. Close to 400 people died in the incidents described above and hundreds more were injured. Fans vent their spleens, fists and weapons on each other as well as on other teams and even on property. At a New York Yankee playoff game, fans threw a softball, a shot glass, a Walkman, a golf ball, plastic bottles, beer cans, a sanitary napkin dispenser, and small change at the opposing Seattle Mariners.[9] At a New York Jets football game at Halloween, a lighthearted bouncing of a Great Pumpkin deteriorated into 41 separate incidents of rowdy behavior and fights.[10] At a Hamilton College ice hockey game, fans threw tennis balls, oranges, apples, melons, two live mice, a dead squid and a life-sized, anatomically correct inflatable doll.[11] The Boston Bruins noticed that the cost of vandalism to the Boston Garden after a win amounts to about $500 whereas the damage after a loss is about $5,000.[12]

The consequences of my booing at the Zippers' championship game weren't all that major, but people killing each other certainly is. It seems there are a lot of people who need a good big sister to convince them to grow up. A fan merging his identity with his team might be emotionally and even spiritually uplifting as he adds his voice to the roar of the crowd that so disturbs the opposing team's offensive line's ability to hear the quarterback's cadence that the guard jumps offside. It's exhilarating to be part of a group of 70,000 – even 100,000 – fans joining together. It makes a fan feel larger than life. When you see sweatshirts with your team's name on them, you feel an affinity for those people from the start.[13]

There's quite a bit of good that can come out of identifying yourself with a larger community. After all, just as there is no "I" in team, there isn't one in "God, Country, and Notre Dame" either. In his marvelous book, *Religion is Not About God*, Loyal Rue demonstrates that one of the evolutionary benefits of being part of a religion is that group membership teaches individuals they can't simply do what they want; they need to stifle self-interest for the good of the community. Thus, while it may not be in an individual Muslim's short-term self-interest to give money to the poor, it's required by the Koran, which makes this "selfless" act into one commended by the group. It also benefits the community as a whole by supporting its vulnerable members.[14]

Similarly, all sports teach the virtue of self-sacrifice. Indeed, sports teach that discipline and sacrifice are the mother's milk of successful team play. Fans know this. They see it. They even demand it. Fans applaud sacrifice and discipline. They may even emulate it in the stands as they respectfully applaud an injured player. That's the good news. 400 people dead and barroom castrations are the bad news.

Like sacrifice and discipline, identity and voice are crucial dimensions of a person's spirituality. It's hard to know how to transcend yourself if you don't know who you are. Both can be used malevolently or benevolently. While identity is an obvious element of spirituality, voice is more subtle. To find their inner identity in fact, spiritual masters (such as St. Ignatius of Loyola or St. Benedict) practiced silence. But voice too is an exercise of one's spirituality and if there is one thing a fan does at a stadium, it is to use voice.

Singing and chanting frequently mark the spiritual practices of religions. Joining in a song, collectively praying and chanting merge us into that larger sense of self whether in church or a stadium. Whether we are joining in an *Agnus Dei* or gesticulating during the *1812 Overture*, we give ourselves over to a larger, collective identity as we merge our voice with others.[15]

Although there are many positives associated with being a sports fan and also negative myths begging to be discredited, it's hard to dismiss the deaths, vandalism and batteries as well as the boorishness and whining. Although I think dead silence might be equally unnerving, fans raising a ruckus and waving their arms behind the backboard of an opposing player's free throw shot is part of the game; deaths and damages should not be.

The difference between the two reflects the maturity of a nine year old who single-mindedly believes a game represents an *us vs. them* contest versus a more balanced approach that appreciates multiple levels of the game. My tiny, rural Stronghurst could teach the presumably sophisticated viewers of today's sports a thing or two about how to really love and watch a game more maturely and richly than a nine year old might. If I just rely on stories of Stronghurst to suggest how to rectify some of our recent problems in sports, however, I'll be dismissed as nostalgic. Fortunately, I can rely on psychological, spiritual and ethical developmental models, which do a pretty good job explaining these small town lessons in contemporary language. I can also rely on Notre Dame.

Western Illinois, where I was raised, does not have a large Catholic population. Rurally Protestant, there were no natural affiliations with the Irish either. Most folks in our area, or at least in our house, liked to cheer for the underdog. In the 1960s, that rarely was ND. There was also the specter of an aunt who taught at Texas when Ara Parseghian's Irish teams were taking on Darrell

Royal's Longhorns in epic Cotton Bowl battles. So I grew up wearing burnt orange, which was also my favorite color.

The games against Texas marked Notre Dame's resumption of playing in bowl games for the first time in more than forty years. Texas, in the midst of a thirty game winning streak, knocked off the Irish in the 1970 Cotton Bowl. I remember nothing about the game except that I was happy. The following year, the Irish ended that Texas winning streak. I remembered that one: I cried.

My brother went to that game and didn't take to the Longhorn fans. In addition, this was a rare time when the Irish were the underdog and Parseghian was a well-liked figure in our house because my father went to Northwestern Law School. Dad really appreciated the life Ara had breathed into the Wildcats before he moved to ND, including their four straight wins over Notre Dame. So my brother cheered – maybe for the only time – for a Notre Dame football team. He thoughtfully brought back a UT tee-shirt, which I wore devotedly, along with a small Irish pin. I gave the pin to one of my Catholic friends.

In fact, had it not been for Parseghian, I'm pretty sure I would have never made it to South Bend. During my junior year in high school, I started looking seriously at colleges to attend via those massive 2,000-plus page college guides. Going to a school in Illinois or a state bordering Illinois was as far as I could comfortably see myself moving from home, but that standard did encompass schools in neighboring Indiana. With a high school graduating class of fifty-five, I could not imagine successfully navigating a giant campus like Ohio State or Michigan, but with only 6,600 undergraduates (at the time) Notre Dame felt manageable.

When I stepped onto campus the first time the summer before senior year, my first thought was, "What am I getting myself into?" My second thought was, "I have to be here!" But I faced two big problems.

ND required two years of a foreign language. Heading into my senior year, I had one year of French. There wasn't a demand for more years of a foreign language in our tiny school, but a lovely teacher gave up her lunch hour for an entire year to teach me and one other student French II. She told us giving up lunch was a blessing because she needed to diet but. I could see she was a generous, dedicated teacher.

The second hurdle was trickier. We were a devout Presbyterian family; my mother was the church organist for over 40 years and she, my father and my grandfather were all elected elders in the church. My grandfather was a Greek major in college, thinking he would become a minister before he decided he didn't have "the call" to become one. So he became a farmer quoting Thucydides in his native tongue while plowing the fields.

While officially supportive of my going to the college of my choice, my affection for Notre Dame perplexed my parents and others, especially since I had toyed with the idea of becoming a minister myself. My parents - conservative, rural Protestants - had a hard time thinking of their son as a celibate priest. They struggled with my desire to go to Notre Dame and were further alarmed when I refused to apply to any other school.

Then my grandfather, fully acknowledged as the spiritual leader of the family and a sports fan to boot, found out that Parseghian, was Presbyterian. Even though he had just stepped down as head coach, it was enough for my grandfather.

"If Ara can do it [at Notre Dame]; Tim can do it too."[16]

That settled the issue.

Notre Dame was – and remains – magical for me. Sure, I was a little weepy-eyed when my parents dropped me off freshman year on my 18th birthday, only to be jarred by the sounds of the Marching Band stepping off to the Victory March. But there are also fabulous memories of games and concerts (I sang in both the Glee Club and Chorale) and wicked snowstorms. All Domers have their own unique memories.

Notre Dame did something very special for me. Its professors and rectors and leaders articulated in a rational, thoughtful way the lessons imbued in me by my parents, siblings, and others on the farm. Notre Dame didn't change my values – it didn't convert me to Catholicism either – but it did supply me with the intellectual capacity to understand and convey those values. To my surprise, once I got underneath some of the rituals and ecclesiology that separated different Christian denominations, the values I found at ND couldn't have resonated more.

When I was a senior, I took Father James Burtchaell's "Theology of Grace." Burtchaell had been Provost when I began my freshman year and was a demanding professor, but "grace" was a Protestant idea (or so I thought) and I couldn't resist spending some time my senior year being grilled by a famous professor. We ended up having long conversations about the old "faith" versus "works" debates that have historically polarized Christian denominations. I could see the different emphases, but thought that insisting on one over the other missed the point. Burtchaell agreed and though it was a tiny thing, his request for me to open the last class of the term with a prayer was one of the most important moments of my Notre Dame career.

Indeed, I found being a Protestant at Notre Dame utterly liberating. At many schools, you are supposed to keep religion out of polite conversations. Happily, that idea seemed foreign to ND's culture, where spirituality was a natural thing to discuss. It was even more interesting playing the gentle protagonist trying to figure out differences and commonalties. Maybe I am giving myself too much credit, but I'd like to think that my questioning role was helpful - it certainly was for me – so much so that I created a scholarship for non-Catholics to attend ND.

The same positive dynamic existed in the Glee Club. My senior year, I served as president. At the beginning of each rehearsal and concert, the President leads the Club in the Hail Mary. I had no problem with the first part of the prayer, but "Holy Mary, Mother of God…" didn't sit well with my Calvinist sentiments.

"You guys need to know I just can't really pray that," I said. But after one of my fellow singers noted that the president simply says the first part and everyone else responds with the part I was uncomfortable with, I decided there were more important issues than the daily liturgical division of speech.

And so, like the proverbial convert becoming more Catholic than the Pope, I found my love of Notre Dame to be so deep exactly because I confronted it with fresh, foreign eyes and was utterly smitten by the place.

All of this exists, as it does for most people who attended Notre Dame, well before the Irish take the field. It makes cheering for the Irish all the more intense and appreciation for Notre Dame solid, regardless of the final score.

I do cheer like crazy for the Irish to win. I once knocked the wind out of myself watching us holding on to beat Missouri in the 1980s and have yelled myself silly on innumerable occasions. But cheering for the Irish to win a football game is not why I kiss the ground when I return to campus. I kiss the ground far more for what happens *outside* the Stadium; those are the real reasons ND is #1.

I'm hardly alone in my reverence for the school. Domers are amazingly loyal. Yes, the prominence of the football team, especially with the NBC contract, does encourage alums around the world to follow the team's progress. One of the greatest traditions of my life is that every bi-annual election night since 1980, I have a conference call with my three college roommates. We talk about the election for about ten minutes, the football team for ten minutes and then catch up with each other. Sports, like the weather, provide a common point of departure. While sports are important, they are the icing on the cake rather than the cake itself.

One scholar has written rather compellingly that sports teams fill the gap created by societies that are big, impersonal and alienating.[17] His analysis builds on the writings of Robert Putnam and others who claim that we no longer have the neighborhood-like affections that provide us with a sense of belonging and identity. Instead, people move around the country and live in cities and suburbs where neighbors don't know each other and turn on the TV or Internet for entertainment rather than engage with the folks next door.

As someone who has used these sociological arguments in my classroom, I understand their power, but

I have also seen them applied too uncritically. I do think, however, that our sports teams can fill this identity-related void a bit. People have always loved sports, of course, but being a fan provides a ready alternative to Putnam's bowling clubs of yesteryear.

Now if you are still in touch with your big sister, you may still have that sense of community even if you are geographically apart. Communities come in different forms today than they did in the 1950s when bowling clubs flourished. Whatever the shape and form, however, individuals still have social needs that are filled by some kind of a community. And what communities do is teach individuals how to see the world and how to act in it.

Thinking that sports may fill these needs can be a problem. Sports are entertaining, but entertainment does not necessarily teach in-depth lessons of community. If we model behavior on sports figures, we replicate actions without community. That superficiality can amplify boorishness (which does have an entertainment value) on television, leading us to conclude that it's normal behavior.

But let's not forget that sports, like business and religion, can be a force for bad *and* good. Like leaving war to the generals, sports are too important to be left to the talking heads on ESPN or even to those they cover. They can teach us some very profound things, even some connected to religion and spirituality. There is a spate of books analogizing religion and sports from both the secular/psychological side and the religious/theological front. Sports fandom can be a kind of spirituality that allows us to transcend a narrow sense of self-interest. That's worth thinking about.

We need communities, but it is useless to yearn nostalgically for imagined days when baseball fields were being built in Iowa cornfields. Teams – sports, neighborhoods, companies, religions – can provide community. Not only that, *every school should be able to explain how God made it #1 – and not just in the season-ending polls. I believe Notre Dame is a great example to show other schools their own divine spark.*

There are both sacred and secular models of ethical and spiritual development.[18] There is some theology in this book, but I am going to try to keep most of it *sotto voce*. Domers, most with a Catholic heritage, should be able to spot this easily, even when explained by a non-Catholic. The message is the same for all: Domers know God Made Notre Dame #1 and because of that, fans of other schools can see the ways in which God made their schools #1 as well.

Us vs. them spirituality represents the belief that "our side" is good and the other side isn't. We find this often in war, where enemies aren't just opponents, but are viewed as having some evil dimension that must be eliminated. Less violently, fans in an *us vs. them* mode see all their team's actions as justified and the other side is lucky or cheating. A Notre Dame fan believing that "God Made Notre Dame #1" might well think that the Almighty actually wills a field goal over the uprights to win the game. On the other hand, a call that goes against your favorite team might raise conspiracy theories about the duplicity of Pac 12 or Big 10 referees.

The next stage is about **respect for the rules of the game** because without rules, you don't even have a game; it's just a bunch of people running around and eventually slugging each other. This level of spirituality is about respect for the officials – even when they screw up. It is also about respect for those rules that makes fans and players call on mystical forces of the universe through superstition and perhaps even by wearing the same magical underwear so that their team continues to win.

The next step is about *sportsmanship, respecting your opponent.* This phase is about seeing the humanity of your opponent, even when that opponent happens to have Down syndrome and is playing the first game of his life, but also when an opponent faces an emotional loss, unfair call or injury. This spirituality treasures not just playing by the rules; it champions a sense of sportsmanship. On the field, this is exemplified when players shake hands at the end of a hard-fought game. In the stands, it's when you pat the fellow in front of you on the back after you've spent the game alternating in primal outbursts of support for your respective teams. You respect each other and your love for your teams and are grateful for a game to enjoy.

The next level is holistic and about love of the *entirety* of the game, when fans sit back and relish the full moment played out before them: the players, colors, bands, stadium, crisp autumn day...the whole works. Fans in this level of spirituality take in not just the score, a fairly played game or the respect of others, but the complete, fun, sun-splashed (or snow-obscured or rain-drenched) moment. This holistic spirituality embraces not just the love of the game, but the love of the sport. Such moments compel us to believe we're part of something that's **as good as it gets** and acknowledge that we're witnessing something unique and special.

The next level is the perspective from the big thing that hangs in the sky during a game: the blimp. If you watch the game from the blimp, you see the game below, but by turning your head slightly, you notice that *lessons of the game apply to other things in life.* Watching a game from the blimp brings a blue-sky perspective on how this game, this day, this sport connect to a wide range of experiences in life. How sport teaches lessons to kids mirrors our politics and how we can apply what we learn in one place somewhere else.

The final level is royal. The Hindu King Arjuna, hero of the Bhagavad-Gita learned that he could engage in battle only by detaching himself from the glories that would result from the battle. Once he had done that, he could participate in battle and not be attached to it. The Bible's King Solomon said there was a time and season for everything under the sun. Life isn't simply about one thing all the time. Different times and situations call for varying responses. Indeed, that's a core theme of the book. Notre Dame isn't about one thing. Even watching a football game doesn't have to be just about one thing. Notre Dame, football and life are about a lot of different things and we can appreciate all of these levels and not just one.

Solomon and Arjuna show us that people can move between different moral and spiritual levels. When it comes to sports, we can engage in blood-curdling cheers for the game-winning field goal and we can also value a well and fairly played game. Sometimes we only scream and sometimes we only value a well and fairly played game. And sometimes, these all happen at once. Regardless of the sequence, each spirituality has its time and season.

A central aim of this book is to explain how these levels of spirituality play out. Remember, I am an ethics professor. I long ago learned that lecturing people about ethics is death to the subject itself. Instead, I've found that we may learn more about how we conduct ourselves –and how we could or might conduct ourselves – if we think about areas of life where we can talk about what we value without becoming defensive. Sports is one of those areas. I'd like to draw you into thinking about how we can appreciate sports by viewing them through different sets of lenses: ***us vs. them, respect for rules, sportsmanship, as good as it gets, a view from the blimp, and the times and season.*** Those different perspectives shed light on other ways we engage life itself. Moreover, I think that Notre Dame provides a great starting point for this approach because Domers are trained to be open to spiritual perspectives. By exploring how these spiritual levels apply to ND and to the Irish, we don't trumpet some superiority over other places; we instead invite others to see these spiritual dynamics play out within their own schools and teams, both inside the stadium and beyond.

***

OK. So much for an ecumenical spirit. Let's get serious and see how God *really* made Notre Dame #1!

The attitudes with which we approach sports allegiances mirror the devotion we often apply to religion. Religion, at its Latin root *religare*, means "to bind." Religion binds people together in a common purpose, even in the midst of sometimes violent competition, with other faiths. Religion makes us into a community; one version of community is a *team*. Both teams and religion require discipline and loyalty. If you are going to be a member of either community, certain rules follow.

Teams and religions create incentives for being a good member, such as punishment for straying from obligations and celebration of commitment. In the end though, as anthropologist Emile Durkheim wrote, religions (and I'd add teams) generate a spirituality that transcends the individuals' interests in the community. Connecting with that transcendence touches the emotions. It generates passion and energy. At its best, it unleashes joy and love.

The thrill of that full engagement, of being part of something bigger than yourself, can be exhilarating and build tremendous confidence. Players know this. Like many fans, I played sports when I was a kid - football, baseball and I ran track all the way through high school. We won a lot, so I was fortunate enough to feel success, pride, and exhilaration. More importantly, we developed camaraderie and affection for each other, so much so that we felt engaged with something bigger than ourselves. All of this gave us great confidence.

We believed in miracles too – even before I knew about Joe Montana – so that when we were behind by a touchdown with only a minute to go and seventy yards from the end zone with our starting quarterback injured, we still thought we'd win the game that decided the conference championship over the LaHarpe Eagles. And we believed when our back-up quarterback, Mike Schmitz, heaved the ball sixty yards to Mike Corzatt, who superhumanly dragged two defenders ten yards across the goal line. We were excited, but hardly shocked.

We also believed the following year in another game that decided the conference championship. Our opponent pushed us around for awhile, the first team to do that to us all year. I knew it was time to make a play. I read the eyes of the quarterback and the receiver I covered, suckered them into thinking I was playing off by dropping back a couple of steps, and then sprinted directly to where I thought the quarterback would throw the ball. He threw it right to that spot and I intercepted the pass and ran 101 yards for the touchdown that broke the game wide-open. I never doubted someone would make a play to turn the game around. I *believed* I could make that play and *looked* for the opportunity to make it.

I'm sure many readers have participated in some sort of game or sporting event. Regardless whether or not you ran 101 yards for a touchdown, you may still have been able to experience the deeper relevance of sports in three important ways.

The first occurs when we are the ones who make the play. I remember every instant of that interception-touchdown run and so does every other player who's ever made a special play.

The second is when you watch a teammate make a play rather than doing so yourself. I wasn't involved when Mike Schmitz heaved the ball that Mike Corzatt caught and then struggled to get over the goal line. I watched. I was a special kind of fan at that moment: a teammate. Because Schmitz and Corzatt exemplified grit and determination and never-say-die-no-matter-how-hopeless-it-looks-effort, I consciously tried to make the big play a year later when we were being pushed around by the Avon Trojans. As a fan/teammate, I learned how to prepare for my moment of glory.

The third way is the very small step we take from fans/teammates to fans. I could just as easily apply the Schmitz-Corzatt lesson I witnessed to other areas of my life, such as when a class I'm teaching isn't going well but I hang in there and get the students' attention and make the class work. I've actually done that many times. I learned that lesson as a fan, and have watched those heroic never-give-up plays by Joe Montana (whom I was once mistaken for at Notre Dame, but I'll get to that later) or Tom Brady and a number of other greats. I learned a lot of things playing football, basketball and baseball and running track that have served me well. There are even more lessons, however, that I have learned from being a fan.

The exhilaration of sports can be experienced after all, from the bleachers and couches of fans across the country. In fact, that's the way many of us spend our sports time. Even professional athletes spend far less than half their lives as players; they're fans as well.

Dozens of books draw upon the insights of players and coaches. But *fans* can also observe and even *participate* in some basic spiritual truths about sports. They can watch the game and *watch themselves* to unearth spiritual truths that make a difference in their daily lives. In an age when fans all too frequently sit back and tut-tut when they see an ethical scandal in sports, such as during baseball's steroid debacle, they also need to step up to the plate to take responsibility for the integrity of the game.

Moving forward, Chapter Two examines the various dimensions of spirituality from the perspective a single rivalry: Michigan. I found myself smack in the middle of that rivalry for eleven years, and it became important not only to my teaching career, but to my own spirituality as well. It is rather bracing to constantly hear that people loathe the school you love on a daily basis.

Chapter Three will look at games the way most fans do: by watching what happens on the field. We learn a lot by watching games and listening to the players and coaches who participate in them. If we listen carefully, we might learn a lot more because the lessons from the field are not just about who wins and who loses; there is much more depth to these battles than you might think.

Chapter Four asks the reader to look around where they sit: in the stands. Fans dynamically interact when the game is played; they don't just watch the playing field. They are also rubbing elbows – literally – with other fans. Sometimes those interactions are pretty nasty, as we saw in the stories early in this chapter. Other times, they are, well, beautiful. It's worth pausing to see how we the fans teach each other important spiritual values.

Chapter Five encourages the reader to take yet another step back. I like to call this the view from the blimp. What do we learn by watching what goes on in the stadium that we might apply to our daily lives? After all, if you watch the game from the blimp, only a small turn of the neck will enable you to see City Hall or a church or a business. Are those places different from sports? Could we transfer knowledge from one to the other? What do we learn in the stadium and beyond?

Chapter Six revisits the notion that to every thing there is a season. While each chapter covers each of these spiritual perspectives – us vs them, respect for rules, sportsmanship, a holistic appreciation of the event, and a perspective from the Blimp, -- this chapter waxes a bit more philosophically about how sports teaches lessons we can apply throughout life. Evidence of how we are already prone to do this is in our frequent use of sports metaphors in business, politics, and elsewhere.

Finally, Chapter Seven summarizes just how God made Notre Dame #1. Yes, we win a lot. In fact, we win more than we think. So do other schools. But the fact that Domers may have a sense of *why* and *how* we win might provide insights to others as to why and how they are special too. Rather than making the notion that God Made Notre Dame #1 an arrogant claim, it actually humbly acknowledges the specialness of *all* schools and teams.

Notre Dame is a special place. I believe that by showing how God made Notre Dame #1, we can add to its specialness and lift up Domers and non-Domers alike.

Even Michigan.

CHAPTER TWO

Ground Zero of a Rivalry: As Good As It Gets

On September 20, 1980, Michigan faced Notre Dame, with only three seconds remaining in the fourth quarter. Michigan led 27-26 and was poised to upset the higher ranked Irish when Harry Oliver, a little used place-kicker lined up to attempt a 51 yard field goal. Besides his inexperience (he had only kicked one field goal in his college career and never beyond 40 yards in his entire career), he faced a 15 mile-an-hour wind in his face, blowing south to north, as it had been the entire day. It would take the kick of his life to boot the football through the uprights. An instant before the center, Steve Siewe, snapped the ball to holder Tim Koegel, the wind stopped. Siewe snapped. Koegel put the ball down. Oliver kicked and the ball sailed and sailed and inched over the uprights. Notre Dame won.

Miraculous! How did such luck occur? How did the wind – which had blown all day – suddenly stop for Oliver's kick? How did such an inexperienced kicker nail a field goal that would daunt the best professional kicker's resolve? Was it a meteorological anomaly? Was it pure luck? Or, as many believed, did God favor Notre Dame over the secular Michigan? Maybe Oliver knew. A famous photo captures Oliver, fully extended in his follow-through just after kicking the ball, with his index finger pointed -where else - towards the heavens. In the stands and in the papers the next day, the inevitable conclusion echoed throughout campus and country: God and the Virgin Mary had smiled again on Notre Dame. In his book on the Michigan-Notre Dame rivalry, John Kryk labeled this "The Miracle Game." Irish coach Dan Devine was quoted as saying "I believe Our Lady gave us a special blessing."

I was a first year law student at Northwestern University in 1980 and the Michigan game was the first I attended as a Notre Dame alumnus. The 1980 contest marked the third game in a renewal of one of college football's greatest rivalries. Simply put, Michigan and Notre Dame are the two most successful major college football programs in history. They lead all college teams in most victories and in best winning percentage (though Texas and Nebraska are challenging ND on the second-most wins front). They have the most members of the College Football Hall of Fame. Although located only 150 miles from each other, the schools had not played for decades until the rivalry resumed in 1978 when Michigan beat a Joe Montana-led Notre Dame coming off the 1977 National Championship. Notre Dame gained revenge in 1979. Both of those were good games, but the 1980 game left everyone exhausted because of its closeness and drama. For Notre Dame fans, it was another chance to claim that "God Made Notre Dame #1."

I first heard that claim five years earlier when I decided to go to Notre Dame for college. When I visited the campus my junior year of high school in the summer of 1975, I almost immediately encountered the slogan "God Made Notre Dame #1" on a student's tee-shirt. I later found it on all kinds of shirts, bumper stickers, and cups in the college bookstore. It struck me as a rather bold claim. While my high school football teammates and I did pray before games, we never prayed to win; we prayed to play our best and asked that no one on either team get hurt. The idea that God might actually cheer for ol' Notre Dame was as intoxicating as it was bold. And so I joined right in believing that the Divine (remember, the coach then was Dan *Devine*) would enjoy helping our guys out a bit. As every Notre Dame fan knows, there have been many games when it seemed that wins came rather miraculously. Maybe God did make Notre Dame #1.

In that summer of 1975, after all, Notre Dame was on a tremendous athletic high. Within the previous sixteen months, the football team had beaten Alabama in the Sugar Bowl to claim the national championship (even though Alabama, bizarrely, still claims the title) and the basketball team had ended UCLA's 88 game winning streak and ascended to #1. That moment was one of three times when both a college basketball and football team held the #1 position. The others occurred in 1967 when UCLA's football and basketball teams were top-ranked; Florida's teams repeated the feat in 2007.[19] During the UCLA upset, a fan held a banner that said:

> Dear John Wooden,
> God Did Make Notre Dame #1
> Sincerely,
> Paul "Bear" Bryant[20]

The football team remained in national prominence throughout the 1970s, winning the championship again in 1977. Phelps' basketball teams were in their glory years as well, nearly always in the top ten, often the top five and occasionally #1.

This across-the-board excellence was hardly a one-off. In 1971, I was in tears when the football team knocked off #1 Texas, the basketball team beat #1 UCLA and the hockey beat #1 Denver, all in just 23 days.[21] With such major wins in prominent sports, you could understand why supernatural claims ensued.

Campus architecture seemed to reaffirm the claim. How many places can say that the Son of God signals a score in a football game?[22] Or has a statue of

Moses also proclaiming #1 status? [23] Or has a statue of the one of its early presidents signaling for a fair catch?[24]

The belief that God made Notre Dame #1 appeals to a primal, *us vs. them* spirituality. When we win, we *know* that God is on our side. (Things are more confusing when we lose.) Believing God is on our side is an exhilarating, empowering spirituality and creates its own power.

We release something quite amazing when we carefully tend to the spiritual side of human nature. Claiming Divine favor is a starting point for a very powerful spirituality and a very natural one – a fiery, blazing connection with transcendent power. There are other spiritual perspectives of that Harry Oliver moment too.

If I were watching that famous Notre Dame-Michigan game, I could also look at benefits of the commitment to a game played by the rules. What provides meaning and enjoyment of the game isn't just who wins, but that the game was won fair-and-square. There is an appealing beauty to a fairly-played game. Games *need* rules, otherwise it's just a bunch of running around.

One reason some people aren't interested in football or baseball or soccer is that they don't understand the rules, which transform a bunch of running around into a purposeful contest. Games let us play - something all animals do naturally - and through them, we learn. Without rules to foster and guide our play, as well as channel our aggression, we're liable just to slug each other in the mouth.

Discipline is another dimension of playing by the rules. Every coach who has ever drawn a breath has used those breaths to preach discipline. Notice the verb: preach, which is exactly the right word. Discipline is also a spiritual value; without it, success on just about any field is impossible.

Enjoying a game played by the rules – and a player who is highly disciplined – holds its own merit and is also something to fall back on when it seems the Almighty has switched teams. After all, the elation of a game-winning field goal can be appreciated by the other side. Disappointment tests discipline.

Indeed, in 1994, a fourth quarter comeback allowed the Irish to take the lead over Michigan with less than a minute to go. This time, however, the Wolverines' own inexperienced kicker, Remy Hamilton, like Harry Oliver fourteen years before, booted a last-second 42 yard field goal to win the game.

I watched the game in my apartment in Ann Arbor, then I joined the University of Michigan Business School Dean's reception to welcome new faculty. Not knowing my background, the Dean's wife greeted me marveling at what a wonderful game had just been played. I choked out that it wasn't so great if you were a Notre Dame graduate.

How could God fail me? It's one thing for Boston College (another Catholic school that had beaten ND on a last-second field goal the previous year) to get God's favor to win a game over the Irish, but the University of Michigan is about as secular a college as one can imagine. How does Blue beat the Irish with a huge field goal at the end of the game? Yes, I know the Lord works in mysterious ways, but what does that do to the idea that God made Notre Dame #1?

As I learned in my next eleven years as a professor at Michigan, the Wolverine alumni weren't as explicit about God smiling on Blue fortunes, but neither were they unwilling to believe that a sense of transcendent force surged through their winged helmets. They, too, had faith. Not necessarily directly linked to God and the Virgin Mary, as Notre Dame fans did, but a faith nonetheless.

So maybe God did make Notre Dame #1. But maybe God made Michigan #1 too. And Texas; maybe God made it #1 too. Texas holds the third most wins and third best winning percentage in college football history. Because my aunt taught there for nearly twenty years, a full-sized regulation UT helmet decorates my office alongside Notre Dame's, Michigan's (and Northwestern's and Indiana's, which aren't close to the top of any football milestone, but with which I do have affiliations). Maybe God made *all* of them #1.

Maybe God doesn't favor any one school over any other but instead wants to favor *every* school. Maybe "God" is more of a spiritual essence permeating all living beings. By believing that essence exists, we enhance our ability to transcend what we think to be our own abilities. Belief allows us to transcend.

We consciously transcend spirituality at different times and places. My "us vs them" spirituality may have been crushed by the Wolverines' field goal, but I soon realized how the Michigan-Notre Dame tradition was itself a thing a beauty. The schools have a good (although not perfect) record of playing by the rules. If you have a profound love of the game itself, you can only relish Notre Dame-Michigan. It is, as a tee shirt before the 1998 game proclaimed, "As Good As it Gets."

A fan in the *as good as it gets* level of spirituality stops for a moment and takes in the entire event. Not just the score. Not just a fairly-played game. Not just the respect for the other team and its fans, but the entire, fun, sun-splashed (or snow-obscured or rain-drenched) moment we've experienced. *As good as it gets* spirituality embraces the love of the game, or even more accurately, the love of the sport.

On an early September day in the Upper Midwest, national television cameras abounding, the enthusiasm of the new school year (and football season) starting, the Notre Dame-Michigan game is *as good as it gets*. One doesn't have to cheer for either team to relish the entire spectacle of a Notre Dame-Michigan game. I might have my *us vs. them* spirituality crushed by the winning Michigan touchdown with eleven seconds to go in 2009, but I could relish the entire *as good as it gets* day.

Being squarely in the middle of the rivalry as a Notre Dame alumnus teaching at Michigan for eleven years helped me see lessons that spilled over to the outside world as well.

It's not so much that God made Notre Dame #1, but rather that Notre Dame fans might have enough faith to believe in a God active in their lives. That confident tee-shirt slogan is more profound than it may first appear. It's not that God rigs a game for a favored team to win, but that a confidence in an active transcendent Force makes that team more powerful. Nor is the experience of that power limited to a scoreboard. What I do – and what you, the reader does – in daily life is as important as Harry Oliver's (or Remy Hamilton's) field goal.

Before we get all cuddly with the Wolverines though, let's remember that ND-Michigan *is a rivalry*. At the risk of writing a book via tee shirt slogans, I bought a shirt from Michigan's M-Den shortly after the recent series in 2014 that said it nicely: "Rivalries Never Die" with the helmets from the two schools facing each other. As any committed fan will tell you, being in the middle of a rivalry means that one is *part* of the rivalry.

For me, the rivalry existed before and after I was a professor at Michigan. The schools had not played each other in thirty years when the on-field rivalry resumed in 1978. In a tradition now gone (sadly, but safely), the students would form a tunnel for the team to take the field before the big home game of the year. Typically, that would be the USC game, but in 1978 (with USC scheduled to be played in Los Angeles), the resumption of the Michigan series made that game a natural.

My roommate was fired up and went charging down the bleachers to take the field. Unfortunately, poised between the stands and the field was the Michigan Marching Band. No problem for "Mace," who barged right through the band, nailing a sousaphone player in the back. The sousaphone player decided to get even with the next guy coming through, which happened to be me. Thus, I can say that I spilt blood when the series resumed.

I also came close to self-immolation. In 1990, my season's seats were in the north end zone on the small bleachers that used to be set up on the field. I had received a new hand-held TV, still a novelty at the time, as a gift so I could watch the replays. Unfortunately, the batteries ran out quickly, so I jammed replacement batteries in my pockets at home, then added some loose change from my mandatory bratwursts just before the game.

About thirty minutes before kickoff, my pants seemed a little warm. Then, they seemed *very* warm. A few minutes later, I thought they were about to catch on fire, they were so hot. I realized that some copper pennies were connecting the batteries in my pockets. I think my jeans would have actually caught fire if I hadn't figured out what was going on.

The rivalry became more interesting when I settled into my job at Michigan. The game was always intense, but I figured I should try to cheer for the Wolverines. I tried for eleven years. While I was able to react benignly to a Michigan win, I could never quite control my glee in a Michigan loss.

At the end of my first year on the faculty, I attended Michigan's spring football game/practice. It was a cold day but there were still 35,000 or so people in the stands. Bob Griese, the reason I wore #12 in my high school playing days, snuck in shortly after I did. His son Brian was battling for quarterback time. (He later led Michigan to the 1997 championship.) I thought about saying hello, but I realized he was just trying to be a dad.

At a juncture in the scrimmage, I stood up and yelled, "Go Wolves!"

The people around me stared at me like I had three heads. I quickly learned that you could yell, "Go Michigan" or even "Go Wolverines." The preferred cheer was "Go Blue." I never again heard anyone in my eleven years at Michigan yell "Go Wolves."

I failed my first test as a Michigan Man. I quickly failed my second one as well.

I received a call from head football coach Lloyd Carr's office the following fall. The young woman on the other end of the phone said she had heard I was a huge college football fan and asked if I would be willing to meet with high school recruits when they visited campus.

"I would love that!" I said.

She said she would get back to me soon with proposed dates. As an ethics professor – a *Notre Dame-trained* ethics professor at that – I felt I had to share a piece of valuable info.

"Just out of curiosity," I asked, "has anyone told you *why* I am a big college football fan?"

"No," she responded. "We just heard that you loved college football."

"Oh, I do," I said. "But you should know that one of my alma maters is one of Blue's biggest rivals and the other is on its way to the (Northwestern's 1996) Rose Bowl. I'll say great things about Michigan; I love it here and it's a great place. But a recruit is going to see my ND and NU helmets on my desk and I'm going to say good things about them as well."

I never heard from Lloyd Carr's office again, though I always teased the folks at Michigan that they had to turn to a Domer when they needed help with ethics.

A few years later, a Notre Dame graduate in my MBA class came up to me with "an ethical dilemma" the week before the annual showdown. The student lived in a house owned by a man who occasionally worked for the Michigan football team and attended practices. According to the student, the house owner was a bit of a blowhard and loudly told a few folks that Michigan had noticed the Irish were not protecting against the onside kick on kickoffs. Michigan had been practicing on onside kick all week and planned to use it during the game.

"What should I do?" the student asked.

"Well," I said, paranoid that our conversation might be under surveillance, "I am an employee of the University of Michigan and I like my job a lot. So I don't believe I should directly undermine the team's preparations for a game with confidential information.

"However, if I were a graduate of ND and a student, rather than an employee of Michigan, and I had the information you just told me, I'd be on the damn phone to the football office in South Bend in ten seconds!"

I don't know if the student actually made the call or not. But I when I watched the game, I waited for the onside kick and noticed that ND *did* protect against it and that Michigan didn't try it. Alas, one year later, Michigan did successfully recover an onside kick.

I believe being a fan of Notre Dame helps me be a better teacher. When the players head out of their locker room, they slap a plaque that says, "Play Like a Champion Today." My wife had a duplicate sign made for me that says, "Teach Like a Champion Today." I slap it on my way to my classes. Teaching students how to be ethical in their business careers is as important as Harry Oliver's and Remy Hamilton's field goals. I learned that *as a fan* and it makes a difference in my job.

When former Notre Dame coach Lou Holtz talks about success, he talks about rules, discipline and incentives. He also talks about love and trust. When teammates love and trust each other, they transcend their individual abilities because they connect with something greater than themselves. Former Michigan coach, the late Bo Schembechler, related his commitment to his team like this: if the President of the United States calls, take a message. When one of my players calls for me, interrupt me immediately.

These messages of commitment, loyalty, love and trust minimize ego and maximize service to each other. They create faith in each other. Religions frequently deify these same attributes. They are characteristics of a loving, benevolent spirit: of God. In the major world religions – Hinduism, Islam, Christianity, Taoism, Judaism and the more philosophical Buddhism – these traits are found in the ultimate source of creation. Whether these attributes fully capture each religion's understanding of their God or not, they capture a dimension of the divine in every faith that allows us to positively and successfully transform our humanity.

When we lived in Ann Arbor, my wife enjoyed wearing Notre Dame sportswear to the local sports gym. She really decked out in Irish gear after a ND win over Michigan. I cautioned her that in a series like Notre Dame-Michigan, each team wins about half the time, so she was setting herself up for payback. Rivalries are rivalries because Harry Oliver kicked a game-winning field goal one year for Notre Dame and Remy Hamilton kicked one for Michigan another year. Teams in rivalries break each other's hearts.

When the series resumed the year after Notre Dame's 1977 National Championship with Joe Montana at quarterback, many thought the Irish would have another great season. Final Score: Michigan 28 Notre Dame 14. Twenty years later, the first team Michigan played after its 1997 National Championship was the Notre Dame Fighting Irish. With Tom Brady at quarterback, many thought that Michigan would have another great season. Final Score: Notre Dame 36 Michigan 20.

Results like this generate emotion and test loyalty and respect.

When I taught at Michigan, I *always* wore ND-emblazoned clothing the Monday after a game, even when Michigan hammered us 38-0 in 2003. At first, students and others in Ann Arbor smirked, but their attitude shifted when I said "I wear ND colors when we win and I wear 'em when we lose." The respect I had for my alma mater as a fan made a fierce rival respect me *and* the rival. It changed the conversation from "us vs them" all the way to "as good as it gets" in about five seconds. That wouldn't have happened if I had hidden my loyalties after a bad game. My Michigan friends and I cheered passionately for our schools, but we also had profound respect for each other's commitment to their school. As I told my Michigan students, I never turned my back on my alma mater and I expected them to follow the same practice.[25]

Connecting one's faith – whether explicitly religious or more non-denominationally spiritual – to one's work, for instance, offers an important lesson. Believing that something about our work transcends us provides incredible possibilities for motivation. It also makes work a lot more meaningful, and if channeled in the right way, can create a whole new approach to the way we run our businesses, churches, governments and other organizations.

Let me give you an example of how this spiritual dimension connects to, but differs from discipline and reward systems both in business and when we work with others in our neighborhoods, churches, schools, and sports leagues. Even if Notre Dame and Michigan weren't the two most successful major college football programs in history, the game would be worth going to each year simply to hear the best two school songs played all day long by the bands.

The great "March King," John Philip Sousa, called Michigan's *The Victors* the best college march ever written. Legend has it that during the Vietnam War, U.S. prisoners of war would hum the Notre Dame Victory March to lift their spirits: it was a song they all knew. While other schools have stirring songs as well, I just don't think you can beat Notre Dame's and Michigan's.

The bands have a neat tradition. During the pregame show, they first play the *other's* school song. So Notre Dame plays Michigan's T*he Victors* and Michigan plays *The Notre Dame Victory March*. I use this example in my ethics classes to show students there is a difference between following the rules, providing incentives for good behavior and simply doing the right thing because it brings its own enjoyment and reward. The marching bands have always provided a concrete example of these points because their rendition of the songs demonstrates the difference between rule-following, being rewarded for doing the right thing and a third, spiritual dimension.

First, the band will politely follow all the *laws* of music, playing in the right time signature, key signature, orchestration, and rhythm and will be rewarded for its actions. The fans whose band just played aren't going to boo and neither are the fans whose song was just played. The audience will politely clap for the politely-played rendition.

When the band plays its own song, however, it plays with heart, pride, and passion. The song becomes a completely different piece of music and sends chills up and down your spine. This rendition is an embrace of the *affective* part of human nature. While human beings practice good behavior in order to avoid punishment or receive an external reward, they also *like* to do good things. Research shows that it elevates certain hormone levels that make us feel good.

This book is about the affective. It is about how to encourage the passion and spirituality that makes not just for polite behavior, but *excellence*. It is about showing how sports players and sports fans regularly tap into something bigger than themselves and what occurs when that happens.

I took my ten-year-old son to the last Michigan and Notre Dame game - at least in the modern iteration of the rivalry - in 2014. He had attended one previous game, the 2013 opener against Temple, a good introduction. As we walked around campus before the game, I began to get texts and emails from my former Michigan students. They were not taunting me, though I knew who they were cheering for. (They better know not to turn their backs on their alma mater!) Instead, everyone hoped I enjoyed the game because they knew how much I relished the entire atmosphere.

Indeed, at the Bookstore, I stopped and talked with several Michigan fans and asked them if they were enjoying themselves and if they were being treated OK.

"Absolutely," they said. "We're kind of surprised just how welcoming everyone is here."

I told them that's the way ND fans generally are.

The stadium filled up early and Steven fully expected that we would be standing and cheering from the moment the band took the field through the first play from scrimmage.

Then he sat down. He turned and looked to me and asked "Dad, why isn't everyone sitting?"

"Steven," I laughed, "this is the MICHIGAN game. I don't think anyone is going to be sitting down, except maybe during commercials and at halftime, for another three and a half hours." By the look on his face, I think he was a little surprised at the intensity.

While Notre Dame has other, greater rivalries than Michigan, even before I had a dual affiliation, I thought that Notre Dame-Michigan was as good as it gets. It had it all: great history, great programs, backyard bragging rights; arguably the leading Catholic university and public university in the country, iconic songs, helmets, coaches and stadiums. How could a rivalry get any better? Still, I relished other rivalries, in part because of my affiliations.

Notre Dame-Northwestern was never a huge rivalry, but the Wildcats have pestered the Irish on more than a few occasions. In addition to the early-sixties Ara streak, there was the 1995 upset that propelled NU to its Rose Bowl. In fact, it was the only time that I got into a verbal altercation with another fan at a game. That fan, who honestly didn't have a clue as to what football was about, started loudly criticizing Lou Holtz as the game wore on. We needed to fire him right away, he said. While it was true we were coming off a subpar (for Holtz teams) 1994 season and were getting upset by the kids from Evanston, I told the guy he was preposterous and that "we will rue the day that Lou Holtz is not on that sideline." I wonder if the guy remembered our conversation as the 90s rolled on.

Although I was disappointed with the Irish loss, I did relish cheering for Northwestern a few weeks later when they did the same thing to Michigan. In fact, my guest at the game kept his head as low as he could in case the Michigan fans surrounding us took out their frustration on my exuberance at the outcome.

When we were living about five blocks from NU's campus and Northwestern (where I received my two terminal degrees) incomprehensibly pulled out a win against ND in 2014, I told my family that my purple alumni hat was pleased, but I identify more with the Gold alumni hat, and it was crushed.

Games aside, Notre Dame and Northwestern get a lot of #1 votes as places that do it right. They educate their players and for the most part comply with NCAA rules. When they play, it is another example of as good as it gets, regardless of what happens on the field.

The same holds true with Stanford. While it's a bit of a reach for me to claim an affiliation, I have published two books with Stanford University Press and am very proud of being a Stanford author. (I published with Yale University Press too, but since we haven't played Yale since 1914, I don't think that much counts.)[26]

I currently teach at Indiana University. Frankly, I thought there would be more of a rivalry with IU than there is. There are a few folks who still growl about Notre Dame stopping play against the Hoosiers fifty years ago, but for the most part, the joke in Bloomington is the reversible jacket folks wear: during the fall, the jacket is worn so that Notre Dame appears on the outside and then it reverses for basketball season to show the cream and crimson colors. Whenever I go for a run, I never get demeaning calls for wearing ND stuff, as I have elsewhere; I get nasty comments for wearing Northwestern's! Imagine that.

Spirituality, at least I am using the term, is about how we connect with the deepest sources and powers of the universe and how we connect with something larger than ourselves. When we do, we transcend the routines of our daily lives and obtain meaning. We also comprehend our ethical duties and the opportunities for moral excellence. Religions articulate those things. So too, in different times, places and ways do philosophy, music, art, poetry, mysticism, and yes, even sports. God Made Notre Dame #1 by making us all #1; it's just a matter of being willing to accept that divine endorsement.

CHAPTER THREE

On the Field:
What Players and Coaches Teach Us

In 2017, my current employer, Indiana University, let go of its basketball coach, Tom Crean. *Sports Illustrated* interviewed Crean in his home a few days later as he and his family started to clean out closets and bookshelves; the reporter noted that the only emotion demonstrated was when Crean gave his cleaning lady Julia a big hug. I laughed because she cleans our house too.

Knowing what was on my sons' bookshelves (mine too), Julia brought over dozens of books written by and about sports figures – books about Ara Parseghian and John Wooden as well as one about how to win with your teammates first before trying to beat an opponent and other values that abound in sports. There was also one featuring Jesus as a coach!

None of this should be surprising. Fans (and readers) want to hear stories from coaches and players. They learn from their heroes and want to read their insights. Whether they are role models or not, coaches and players do have a unique platform to teach values and share stories. Notre Dame does not take a back seat to anyone in the stories its players and coaches can tell and the values they followed.

The year after ND won the national championship over Texas in the Cotton Bowl, the Irish returned to face the Houston Cougars. A huge ice storm hit the Dallas area before the game, turning the metropolitan area into an ice rink. With wind chills below zero and, by game's end, a nearly empty stadium, the Irish played a miserable game. Quarterback Joe Montana suffered from the flu and ended up eating chicken soup in the locker room wrapped in blankets as the Irish found themselves down 34-12 with less than half of the final quarter to go.

For the second year in a row, I attended the Cotton Bowl with some fellow ND students. One of them had been in an automobile accident years before and still needed crutches to walk. The circulation in his legs was poor as well. We didn't have a handicapped decal for my car –I'm not sure those decals were even around at that time – but we explained Mike's situation to a very understanding traffic guard at the entrance of the Cotton Bowl. With most of the crowed staying home because of the weather, the guard allowed us to park right next to the stadium entrance, just steps from our seats.

None of us expected Dallas to treat us to subzero wind chills, so we were poorly dressed. We stayed in the stadium throughout the first half though, hoping for things to turn around. We were getting awfully cold though, and Mike's legs were literally turning blue. So at halftime we went to the car and warmed up. We thought about returning for the second half kick-off, but Mike's legs told us that we should stay put, listening to the game on the radio.

We were still there in the fourth quarter when we heard the play-by-play of Tony Belden's blocked punt and Steve Cichy's return for a touchdown as well as a quick follow-up touchdown by Montana to cut the Houston lead to 34-28. At that point, we scrambled back into the stadium, led by Mike, to see if another ND miracle was about to unfold.

Initially, it looked like our re-entry into the stadium might be for naught as Montana fumbled the next time we had the ball. But Houston couldn't move in the cold either. Fearing the elements, Houston gambled on converting a fourth-down play on their own 29 yard line. When the Irish defense stopped the Cougars, Montana had twenty-eight seconds left. He scrambled for eleven and completed a pass to Kris Haines for another ten with just six left. An incomplete pass left just two seconds, but then Montana hit Haines for a touchdown to tie the game with no time remaining. Kicker Joe Unis completed the extra point (on two tries after the first one was nullified on an offsides penalty). The Irish had completed a miraculous, stunning comeback.

Comebacks like this make fans claim their team is #1. Against all odds, in improbable conditions, and with a drama Hollywood could not imagine, your team wins. You conclude there must have been some divine magic at work. There's more than that. We fans want to find a way to find a connection to these players and coaches. Why else would someone wear a jersey that says "Montana" on the back of it? Actually, with the possible exceptions of Montana or the Cubs' Ernie Banks, I never wanted anyone else's name on the back of my jersey; I wanted my own name back there. Yet people buy millions of jerseys with names on the back so they can have a little of that Montana connection. That same desire holds true for autograph seekers and hand shakers who desperately want that connection. In that respect, I'm very similar and though I never met Joe Montana, I can say I have a unique connection to him.

In my last year of high school, Montana had a couple of big comeback wins for the Irish, so there was a buzz about him, but he wasn't the starting quarterback yet. In my freshman year at ND, he was out for the year with a shoulder problem. Since this was well before social media, there were not many photos of the players available, so there was some mystery as to exactly what Montana looked like.

That became clear when I was sitting on the porch of Sorin Hall, wearing my old high school football jersey. My number 12 originated when I had dreams of quarterbacking, but those dreams gave way my senior year to being a wide receiver on offense and cornerback on defense. My number 12 was still a quarterback's number though, and my arm was in a sling from a baseball injury. And even though I was 5'8" rather than Montana's 6'3," the rest of the image fit.

"Hey, are you Joe Montana?"

Had it been a cute girl from the neighboring Walsh Hall, I might have said yes.

I've always loved telling the story, especially as Montana became a larger-than-life figure at both ND and in the NFL. In fact, the best venue for telling the story is when I teach the NFL players and challenge them to guess what NFL Hall of Famer I was once mistaken for. To say they are stumped would be an understatement. They can't fathom any NFL player – Hall of Famer or not – that I would ever be mistaken for. Even these NFL players have a desire to be like – and have a connection with – a legend like Montana.

Some guys just have "it." Montana sure did. Some schools also seem to have "it." Notre Dame sure does. Miraculous wins give an aura to people and schools and the hyperbole begins.

Many times, the Irish pull out wins or throw down performances that seem superhuman, such as when the Four Horsemen upset Army in 1924. That game, which led the Irish to Knute Rockne's third national championship, sparked one of the most famous sports columns in history when *New York Herald Times* writer

Grantland Rice referred to them as a "wild horse stampede," alluding to them in mystical terms and boosting a larger-than-life aura.

> Outlined against a blue-gray October sky, the Four Horsemen rode again. In dramatic lore they are known as Famine, Pestilence, Destruction and Death. These are only aliases. Their real names are Stuhldreher, Miller, Crowley and Laden. They formed the crest of the South Bend cyclone before which another fighting Army football team was swept over the precipice at the Polo Grounds yesterday afternoon as 55, 000 spectators peered down on the bewildering panorama spread on the green plain below.[27]

Another game that made fans claim divine intervention was the Irish upset of Ohio State in 1935 after the Buckeyes had jumped out to a 13-0 lead. The Irish team's captain Joe Sullivan had died before the year began and the team said a prayer for him before every game. That, a remarkable performance by second stringer Joe Pilney, a 4th quarter touchdown pass from Bill Shakespeare (how many teams have a player named William Shakespeare!), and a play from a fourth-stringer who was only at the game because he snuck onto the team bus and hid in a teammate's train berth, led to a win some call "the first game of the century."[28]

Nearly twenty years later, the Irish pulled off another enormous upset when they ended Oklahoma's 47 game winning streak in 1957. According to Monty Stickles, a starter for the Irish, the team went to mass that morning and met a group of 8-10 year olds who implored them to win so they would have bragging rights over the Oklahoma Baptists. As Stickles put it, the plea had a "win one for the Catholics thing."[29] Neither team scored until the fourth quarter when the Irish finally found the end zone on a fourth down call. Rather than pounding the ball up the middle, quarterback Bobby Williams faked an off-tackle handoff to Nick Pietrosante and pitched the ball instead to Dick Lynch who ran around the corner into the end zone.

The first time I remember actually pulling for Notre Dame was in the Sugar Bowl against Alabama on New Year's Eve, 1973. Notre Dame's underdog status and Midwestern origin were enough to place the family in the Irish corner for that game. And there was Ara, still beloved from his days coaching Northwestern.

Howard Cosell set the stage. "This is the dream matchup: Notre Dame-Alabama. At Notre Dame, football is a religion. At Alabama, it is a way of life."

The game's 24-23 score with just over two minutes to go denoted just how close the game was. With Notre Dame pinned against its own five yard line, Ara made perhaps his most famous call. A third-down pass play that ended up in the hands of second-string tight end Robin Weber for a 35 yard game that sealed the win and the national championship.

A year and a day later, the Irish and Alabama squared off in the 1975 Orange Bowl. That 1974 season was difficult for the Irish, as preseason hopes were dashed by Purdue. The season finale featured USC's stunning comeback from a 24-0 deficit to beat the Irish 55-24. Parseghian announced that the Orange Bowl would be his last game. Trailing 13-11 in the fourth quarter, Alabama mounted a late drive that looked like it might deprive Ara of a triumphant exit, but a Reggie Barnett interception with a minute to go sealed the win.

These stories don't include the wins over Texas, Michigan and Miami, the upsets over #1 teams like Florida State in 1993 or Pitt in 1982 or other famous games like the Snow Bowl win against Penn State in 1992. When a fan witnesses such wins time and time again, accompanied by lines from the greatest school song ever – *what though the odds be great or small....or shake down the thunder from the sky* – it sure seems something transcendent is in the air.

ND's two longest rivalries, though, give an even richer sense of just how God made Notre Dame #1. Though he had a great start, Charlie Weis struggled in his five years as head coach. Yet Weis did something very special during his tenure: he took an already-hearty respect for Navy and crafted one of the very best Irish traditions.

Played since 1927, the Navy game is the longest uninterrupted rivalry in college football. Though lopsided in won-loss results (the Irish lead the series 75-12-1 and once won 43 consecutive games), the event is cherished by both sides. For Notre Dame, playing the game attempts to pay "an unpayable debt."[30] It is rare to see two schools that so openly respect and admire each other.

Navy helped Notre Dame in two ways. In the 1920s, Big Ten schools, led by Michigan, snubbed Notre Dame and refused to play the Irish. Some Big Ten schools, like Purdue and Michigan State, bucked the ban, and it took its toll on the Irish. That was one reason why Notre Dame began to regularly schedule the service academies, including Navy, starting in 1927.[31]

But there is an even more important reason for Notre Dame's gratitude and for why ND was once called "Annapolis West." During World War II, Notre Dame's enrollments were so low that it was doubtful the school could remain open. The Navy, however, rented campus space for its own training and commissioned scientific experiments. With Navy headquarters located where the Hesburgh Library and Touchdown Jesus currently stand, the Navy coordinated the establishment of Notre Dame as Midshipman Reserve School, which commissioned 25,000 reserve officers and ensigns during World War II. Many of those students took classes taught by ND professors, further helping maintain the core of the university[32] and keeping Notre Dame alive. As a result, ND administrators have said Notre Dame will play Navy as long as Navy wants the game.

When Weis became coach, he took the respect ND had for Navy to the next level by having the team go to the Navy sideline after the game and stand in solidarity with the Midshipman as the Navy Anthem was played. Navy returned the favor, heading to the Irish sideline after the game to hear ND's "Alma Mater." And so a new tradition of respect and sportsmanship is demonstrated at each game. Respect like this can be more profound than rankings in a sportswriter's, coaches', or computer poll.

Is it just Notre Dame that appreciates Navy? Here is the Navy side of things, from a Q&A on its official website:

> Q: Why does Navy continue to schedule Notre Dame in football when Navy has not won a game against ND for 40 years? Navy has come close but still no cigar. -
>
> A: The Notre Dame-Navy series is the longest intersectional rivalry in college football. I don't believe that Navy would ever consider dropping that contest. We have a wonderful relationship

with the institution. It brings national exposure to the program, and it seems every year it's a real great, down-to-the-last-minute contest.

Regardless of wins or losses, it's always a pleasure to be associated with that fine institution, and it makes for a real exciting opportunity for our midshipmen to compete at a very high national level.[33]

When you have a rival like Navy, it's easy to follow them and even cheer for them the rest of the season. I've never met any player, coach or fan who didn't keep his or her eye on what rivals are doing when they play someone else. If you keep your eyes on Navy, you are bound to see them play their greatest rival, Army. As President Dwight Eisenhower once said, "The Army and the Navy are the best friends in the world 364 and a half days a year."[34]

Over time, college football has become more about big schools with NFL-bound players, leaving behind the traditions found in games like Army-Navy. There are many things to learn from the Army-Navy rivalry, and they're not all about football.

Many refer to the annual contest as a family reunion, where the bond between soldiers and their families is witnessed by the world through the lens of college football.[35] These men are used to working like a team—after all, as a military unit, it is imperative that they trust and understand each other. Instead of the possibility of a multi-million dollar NFL contract, these players will serve a mandatory five years, and many will opt for more. For them, the game is not about regular niceties and sportsmanship, but about honor and respect.[36] With a larger "alumni" base than most schools, the institutions generate huge crowds at the stadium and many more listening or watching around the world.

Despite the *Beat Army* slogan and mascot-stealing antics, Army and Navy are two institutions that care quite a bit about rules: what type of haircut you may have, which pin you may wear on which lapel, how long you are permitted to eat—every minute of the day is dictated by rules that must be followed. As a tough Marine in "A Few Good Men," Jack Nicholson famously said, "You follow orders, or people die," death being the ultimate punishment, at least in his character's view, for not following rules.

The Army-Navy game can be greatly affected by current events. In 1967, the game entertained 101,000 fans during the war in Vietnam.[37] Navy captain Bill Dow said he felt like the entire crowd was cheering for both teams united as one, and recounted how he received more than a dozen cards a day from soldiers in Vietnam who were pulling for his team.[38]

Army's 8-1 record in 1967 won them an invitation to the Sugar Bowl, its first bowl bid. When the Secretary of the Army refused to allow them to play the game in wartime, West Pointers showed their disdain for the decision (respectfully, of course) by removing the mess hall's sugar bowls.[39]

More recently, the teams played after the U.S. and Iraq went to war in March 2003. By the time of the game, the Midshipmen were mourning a recent former football player killed in action, a receiver named James Blecksmith.[40] The seniors on the teams began their freshman year a few months before September 11, 2001, and never expected to be fighting a war on terror.[41]

53

"Should I come to your graduation or Army-Navy?" In 2007, Army's middle linebacker, Brian Chmura, had an easy answer for his father, a Lieutenant Colonel with just one leave from Iraq remaining. The younger Chmura let his father know that the Army-Navy game was more important than graduation.[42]

Surely nothing for a Cadet or a Midshipman is more bitter than a loss to the other, nothing more glorifying than a win. But the game offers more than that. The rules alone have their own value, as do the rules of the academies, the game itself, and the rituals of preparation and superstition attendant to watching and playing the game. A football game can be rough, but you'd be hard-pressed to find any conduct other than sportsmanship at an Army-Navy contest.

Army-Navy is special, but it is part of something larger. It's worth remembering the verb used to describe those who participate in a football game. They *play*. Football can capture players' and fans' attention and passion, careers can be made and businesses based on the sport. Yet in the final analysis, this is a game that people *play*.

Take it from Ohio State legend, Archie Griffin, the only two-time winner of the Heisman Trophy. At the OSU Alumni Club, Griffin noted:

> I've heard debates back and forth about how heated some of our rivalries are and how much animosity can flow between fanbases at times. Having heard all of that I've yet to hear a compelling argument that suggests treating other people poorly is ever warranted....

Part of the reason it's always stuck in my craw is that as a player, as heated as our rivalry with Michigan could be, that game was never about hate. We wanted to beat them badly, no doubt aboutit. However, that desire never ever led me or my teammates to engage in the type of crass behavior that would reflect poorly on Ohio State.

When we played the Wolverines the goal was to play as hard as we possibly could. We had to leave it all out there because we knew they were going to do the same. But at the same time, we had to play fair. And when the game was over you walked across the field, shook their hands, and offered them the respect they deserved for testing your mettle on that day.

***

At the end of the day, these are games. We should never get to the point where a game leads us to behave in a way that would embarrass our families or our university. Being a good fan is something to me that is as much of a part of being a Buckeye as Skull Session or Script Ohio. It isn't something I expect out of *some* of our fans. I expect it out of *all* of them wherever they are.[43]

Our rivals – and our rivals' rivals – remind us of the importance of rules and the importance of sportsmanship.

Just as I've never met a coach, player or fan who didn't keep his or her eye on a rival, I've never met one who wasn't interested in other sports. Fall games at Notre Dame Stadium feature updates on teams in a pennant race. Cheers and groans alike can erupt because Notre Dame fans come from all over the country. They may cheer the gold helmets in front of them, but they might also sport a blue Yankees hat, a red Cardinals hat or a yellow A's hat.

In those moments, the Red Sox fan does not cease to be a fellow Domer when seated by a Yankees fan. There is a shared identity that bonds them as Notre Dame fans while they cheer for their favorite baseball teams. We share a common bond even as we follow and cheer separate teams. As a result, the fellow next to you commands your respect because he is simultaneously part of you and different from you.

I think that Notre Dame's national (and international) composition helps Domers recognize that shared bond. Once we claim our Domer identity and recognize the fun that difference and diversity bring, we can more easily celebrate a game in richer ways than just *us vs them*. That respect for opponents is why Notre Dame does a great job celebrating games and printing tee shirts that celebrate the game more than inflicting invective on an opponent.

We learn from other teams and other sports even as we cheer at Notre Dame Stadium or in the Joyce ACC Baseball, tennis and other sports teach us a lot about competition, rules, sportsmanship and the beauty of moments.

Consider the maligned umpire. No one is more prone to the abuses of fans (and players and coaches) than the referees and umpires of our games. Yet they are crucial. Without them, there is not a *game*. Indeed, without rules, there is no game. When a football play ends, players from both teams (usually) return to the huddle. They don't continue to pummel each other. That is because the *game* only gets played by having some rules. So when fans appreciate the *plays* of the *game* they are valuing more than victory; they are appreciating the *game* of football or basketball. The umpires simply enforce the rules so the game continues. For that, they get abused. Indeed, abusing umpires and referees is something of a sick sport unto itself.

In 2010, Detroit Tiger pitcher Arman Gallaraga was close to a perfect game when umpire Jim Joyce mistakenly called runner Jason Donald safe at first base. The replay clearly showed that Donald was out and the right call would have resulted in that rarest of baseball feats: a perfect game.

You might have expected Gallaraga to explode in fury. But he didn't. Nor was Joyce obstinate. Instead, he admitted he had blown the call and apologized for costing Gallaraga his perfect game. Gallaraga graciously embraced Joyce with no hard feelings. Detroit fans cheered Joyce the next day as Gallaraga brought out the lineup card to that day's home plate umpire, Joyce. They embraced and the fans continued to cheer. It was one of baseball's best moments because it demonstrated a respect for the rules and the game as well as sportsmanship by both parties. Joyce admitted he had not properly enforced the rules, which are crucial to baseball and literally define what constitutes a perfect game. Gallaraga's embrace of Joyce made the game even better.

Nine months earlier, a less compelling story took place. Coming into the U.S. Open in September 2009, legendary tennis player, Serena Williams was ranked number two in the world and seeking her 12th Grand

Slam title. There was little doubt that she would emerge victorious after facing the 26-year-old mother of a toddler, Kim Clijsters, who was returning to the game after two years of maternity leave as an unseeded wildcard entry in that year's competition.

Yet Clijsters outperformed her opponent throughout the contest and Williams became visibly frustrated even before the first few games were over. Upon losing the first set to Clijsters, Williams slammed her racket on the ground twice, breaking the racket and earning her a warning for racket abuse.

Clijsters was leading the second set 6-5 when at 15-30, Williams was called for a foot fault on her second serve. She argued with the lineswoman who made the call and returned to the baseline in what seemed like an attempt to go forward with the match. Instead of continuing her serves, however, Williams approached the judge, shook a tennis ball in her face, and threatened her with profane language.

Louise Engzell, the chair umpire, then assessed Williams, who otherwise has had a remarkable career, a code violation. The tournament referee concurred with Engzell's decision. Williams lost the point, which resulted in her losing the match. She was also fined $10,000 for unsportsmanlike conduct and $500 for racket abuse. Williams' outburst ended her journey to the finals. Clijsters went on to win the U.S. Open.

The tournament referee explained the penalty procedures after the match to offer some insight into the unusual result. "It just happened that point penalty was match point."

"To get a point penalty at that time, it's unfortunate," Clijsters recounted after the game. "But there are rules."[44]

Sportsmanship is a step beyond following the rules. Sometimes players treat each other with such decency, you have to tip your hat to them. Sometimes, good sportsmanship can even overcome an official's error, as it did with Gallaraga's actions.

We can find another example of excellent sportsmanship in the 59th minute of the final game of the season, when the Framingham State women's soccer team was awarded a goal to give the team a 1-0 lead over Bridgewater State in a game Framingham needed to clinch the regular season conference title and advance to the postseason tournament. The goal, however, was awarded erroneously, as Coach Tucker Reynolds and a handful of his players saw the ball roll into the side of the net but not *inside* it.

Reynolds gathered his team and instructed them to allow Bridgewater State to score and tie the game. While the team was reluctant to accept the coach's decision, they understood why he made it and knew they would still have a chance to win the game even though the score was about to be tied again.

Wanting to teach a lesson about sportsmanship, Reynolds said, "Most of my players are education majors and will become teachers someday, and most of them also will be parents."

Framingham State wound up losing the game 3-2, and missed out on the conference title as well as the postseason. Reynolds has no regrets and he and his team received words of appreciation from the Bridgewater State players, coaches and supporters.

"Five years from now, nobody is going to know or care what the score of the game was, but maybe somebody's going to be talking to their child about ethics and sportsmanship because of that game," said Reynolds. "There's no greater honor for me as the coach or for them as young athletes to be recognized for something that's probably a little bit more important than the outcome of a game."[45]

Sometimes, good sportsmanship takes your breath away.

In another example, what most high school football players would have considered one of the worst days in their athletic careers was exactly the opposite for one of their teammates. In St. Joseph, Missouri, Benton High School's freshman football team was losing 46-0 to Maryville with only ten seconds left in the game. It was clear that Benton had no chance of winning, but their coach, Dan McCamy, would make good use of those ten seconds. He called his final timeout and approached the opposing team's defensive coach, David McEnaney, while the Benton team prepared for the "Matt play." What McCamy then requested is unheard of in high school sports: He wanted the Maryville defense to let one of his players run in for a touchdown.

Yet Matt Ziesel is no typical high school freshman football player. At 5-foot-3 and 100 pounds, there is little wonder why Ziesel's mother and pediatrician were concerned with him playing such a physically demanding sport. In addition to his less-than-intimidating stature, the fifteen-year-old also suffers from Downs Syndrome. Coach McCamy explained this "special situation" to the opposing team and asked that the players refrain from making physical contact with Ziesel but to be as real as possible for him. With the plan is place, the ball was snapped, Ziesel ran a sweep to the right, and then continued for 60 yards to score his first high school touchdown. McCamy said the Maryville players "jumped right on board" when he requested their help and although Benton lost the game, "When we went away, we were all kind of winners."

Ziesel's touchdown run was posted on the Internet. It didn't take long for it to become a YouTube sensation. Ziesel's parents and Coach McCamy have expressed their amazement with the impact this simple moment has had on their community and the region All three are constantly reminded how important this achievement was for Ziesel.[46]

In a similar scenario, Will Rudolph was a senior at Carmel High School and had spent all four years there as the team manager for the basketball, football and baseball teams. Will had never played in a game at Carmel High School, but his dream was to be in a Carmel High School baseball game even though he suffers from cerebellar ataxia, a mild form of cerebral palsy.

Three weeks before Carmel was to play Gonzales High, Coach Randall Bispo got permission from Will's parents and selected a uniform for Will. With Carmel leading Gonzales 11-1with one out in the sixth inning, Bispo sent Will in as a pinch runner for Alberto Palafox at third base. Will, who hadn't been on base since Little League, took his lead off third, sizing up the pitcher.

Michael Gerlach, the batter, was "rejoicing about the chance to get [Will} in." He hit the ball and ran towards first as Will made a dash for home. Gerlach was mortified to see the third baseman for Gonzales, Manuel Madrid, preparing to throw to home plate but Gonzales catcher Francisco Banuelos was pointing for Madrid to throw to first, hoping his teammate would realize this was no routine play. So instead of throwing home, which would have inevitably gotten Will out, Madrid threw to first. After Will scored, the Carmel High baseball team leapt out of the dugout and hoisted him onto their shoulders.[47] Will's run was the last for Carmel, who won the game 12-1.

Back at the Dome, for thirty-nine years, ND's head coach Digger Phelps and his team played a Christmas season game against Butch Waxman and the Logan Center Olympic Team. Logan Center is located just off the Notre Dame campus and serves individuals with disabilities. Waxman, a resident of Logan Center and frequent guest on the sidelines of Notre Dame basketball during Phelps' tenure, beat ND with a last second shot each of those thirty-nine years. Is there anyone in this paragraph who is not #1?

Embracing the importance of *sportsmanship* and *as good at it gets* doesn't require relinquishing a fierce *us vs. them* battle. It just keeps *us vs. them* in perspective and opens up additional ways to relish a contest, even the fiercest of Notre Dame football battles against USC. In fact, the fierceness of a rivalry can be the bond that unites rivals. There is pride in the rivalry itself. As Anthony Davis – yes, that headache from the Trojans – said to Lou Holtz after Holtz's first USC game, "Welcome to the rivalry."

As fired up as Notre Dame gets about Miami, Florida State, Ohio State or Texas and as long-standing as rivalries may be against Navy, Michigan, Purdue and Michigan State, nothing stands up to the Southern Cal game. It starts with contrasts. While Navy sports the same blue and gold as ND – even the helmets look identical, though Navy doesn't add gold dust – and Michigan's blues and Purdue's gold look like ours, USC's cardinal red stands apart. There is no confusing the sun-kissed west coasters with the Catholic Midwesterners.

Yet they are both glamour schools, each with a claim to eleven national championships, legendary coaches, and great school songs. They are first and second in terms of producing the greatest number of Heisman Trophy winners. This intersectional rivalry dates back to 1926 and has been played every year since.

Competing accounts explain the origin of the series. The most logical is that it made financial sense to schedule an intersectional game between two schools of this caliber. The coaches, Knute Rockne and Howard Jones, had opposed each other when Jones was at Iowa and they were friends. A more colorful story is that a journalist told Jones the series would be good and questioned whether Jones might be afraid of Rockne. Of course, Jones rejected that notion as did Rockne when, allegedly, the journalist pulled the same ruse on him.[48]

An even better story has it that USC athletic director, Gyynne Wilson and his wife travelled to Lincoln, Nebraska, where the Irish were playing the Cornhuskers one November. Mrs. Wilson befriended Bonnie Rockne, convincing her that a season-ending game in warm Southern California would be more enjoyable than a harsh Midwestern closer. Mrs. Rockne, in turn, convinced Knute.[49]

Three games stand out. One was the last game of Holtz's first year, 1986, when the Irish rallied from a 37-20 deficit with just seven minutes to go to pull off a comeback that propelled the Irish on the road back to elite status and the 1988 Championship. Then, in 1988, the game marked the only time the teams met as #1 and #2 with both coming into the season finale undefeated. Making the game all the more intense was the news that

Holtz sent the team's two leading rushers home the night before for disciplinary reasons.

When that news hit, ND fans took it in different ways, but the majority of fans I encountered counted it as a proud moment. With *everything* on the line, Holtz insisted that rules were meant to be followed. Perhaps it is a bit moralistic to tout this style of discipline in the same year as the unfortunate *Catholics vs. Convicts* battle against Miami. The Irish stayed in control throughout the game and cruised to a 27-10 victory. I turned my first backward summersault in twenty years when Tony Rice broke an option down the sideline early in the game to score a 65 yard touchdown. Being a fan can require athleticism too!

Perhaps the biggest Notre Dame win was the famous 1977 Green Jersey Game. Notre Dame had finished the previous season strong, with a win in the Gator Bowl against Penn State. Big things were expected for the 1977 Irish with great experience and talent returning. Many preseason prognosticators had the Irish as the #1 team in the country going into the season. Yet the season started slowly with a poorly-played win over defending champion Pittsburgh. Then came the shocker: an upset against a mediocre Ole Miss team. Suddenly the season was in serious jeopardy.

Things only got worse the next week against Purdue. Starting quarterback Rusty Lisch struggled and was replaced by backup Gary Forystek. Forystek didn't last long, suffering a terrible injury; in one hit, he broke a vertebra in his back, his clavicle, and suffered a concussion. Coach Dan Devine reinserted Lisch, but with Purdue ahead 24-14 and the season on the line, Devine brought in third-string quarterback Joe Montana with eleven minutes to go in the game. Montana threw for 154 yards and led the Irish to a 17 point comeback that saved the season.

The Irish were not yet firing on all cylinders, but with Montana established as the quarterback, the team kept winning and headed into the USC game as the #10 team in the country. USC had been ranked #1, but had been upset the previous week by Washington and so it came into the game at #5 with a record of 5-1.

As always, the campus was rocking during USC week, including at a feverish pep rally in Stepan Center. Digger Phelps, the hottest coaching commodity on campus at the time, told the crowd that, rather than chanting "We are …ND" at the game, we should chant "We are…The Green Machine." Like robots, we did what Digger told us to do, but many of us looked at each other because: (1) we didn't wear green (2) the extra two syllables kind of screwed up the cheer. Several of us thought Digger was off his rocker.

We figured things out the next day when the team returned to the field in their now-famous green jerseys. Most of the student body was on the field forming the tunnel for the team to run through, but unless you were in the first row of the tunnel, it was hard to see the team come out. As we looked up to the stands, the stadium seemed to be a rocket lifting off. Then we heard: "We're wearing GREEN!" Fighting our way to see the players, we caught the green jerseys, as well as USC head coach John Robinson shaking his head at the scene.

The best part of the entire pre-game was when a huge Trojan horse was wheeled out onto the field. Intramural football players dressed in ND gear jumped out of the horse's belly. Unfortunately, they were still wearing blue jerseys, but that was a small matter on the whole.

I'm not sure the Pittsburgh Steelers, then in their NFL glory days, could have stopped us that day. After an exchange of scores, Montana led the Irish to 28 unanswered points. Ted Burgmeier, who had moved to defensive back and was my favorite player on defense, had an amazing game with an interception and a fake field goal run as the holder. Both plays set up touchdowns and then completed a two-point conversion pass after a bobbled snap from center.[50]

The Irish rolled over USC 49-19 on its way to its national championship win against Texas in the 1978 Cotton Bowl.

One other game caught my attention. On the sixth anniversary of the green jersey game, Gerry Faust put the Irish in green again. I went to the game with a girl I had just started to date. She wasn't much of a fan. When I saw the green jerseys, I went crazy.

"Why are you so excited," she asked.

"Because they are in green!" I exuded.

"Yes, they are. So what?"

I tried to explain, but if you are not immersed in ND culture, it is hard to explain why a you'd become ecstatic about some guys wearing green shirts instead of blue.

When Devine took over as head coach, Phelps suggested that the football team wear green jerseys before the 1975 game, but Devine declined as he did the following year when Alabama and Bear Bryant came to town for the first time. By 1977, though, Devine was ready. Digger explained how to pull off the switch:

> First, have the team warm up in their normal blue jerseys...then have the managers put the green jerseys in their lockers while they are warming up. Second, don't tell the players what you are doing, just surprise them. You won't have to say a word. Don't even give a pregame talk, the jerseys will do all the motivating you will need. Finally, make sure Southern Cal is on the field first, even if you have to take a delay of game penalty.[51]

Phelps claims he has a two-foot picture of USC coach John Robinson with his hands on his hips and his mouth wide open, a moment we must have both witnessed.[52]

Though I wasn't a glimmer in anyone's eye in 1935, that contest is also worth noting because of the intrusion of another vital force. The game looked to be an easy one for the Irish. ND headed in with a 6-1-1 record while the Trojans were 1-4, but USC held a 6-0 halftime lead until the band interceded. According to one of the Trojan players:

> We were leading at the half and we came back on the field after intermission...We're holding on, and we're ahead and we walk on the field and they have a band covering the entire
> field waiting for us, and they strike up *Ave Maria* in memory of Knute Rockne. So we all stand at attention, and they play it through twice. It was 18 degrees at South bend... it was soooo cold. In the meantime, the Notre Dame team is huddling underneath a blanket. Well, they

finally kick off to us, one of our guys fumbles the ball at the 3-yard line, and they pick it up…and go in for a score. The damn band beat us.[53]

The Irish went on to a 20-13 victory. Hmm. The fans. The band. The weather. *Ave Maria.* No wonder we Domers think there are forces at play in a game that transcend the grass on the field.

Some have used the divine endorsement of the Irish against us as well.

In 1969, USC was ranked at #3 and the Irish at #5. The game was tied 14-14 when a potentially game-winning Irish field goal hit the crossbar and bounced away with two minutes remaining. "God was a Trojan on that kick," according to USC coach John McKay.[54]

One of the curious things about the ND-USC rivalry is the record of the coaches. To be sure, some of the most iconic coaches in the rivalry have exceptional records. Lou Holtz was 9-1-1 ; Pete Carroll and Frank Leahy were both 8-1-1. But then Ara Parseghian was only 3-6-2 despite his otherwise glittering record in South Bend. Dan Devine struggled even more at 1-5. John McKay had a lot to do with Ara's record, but McKay was only 8-6-2, in large part because Joe Kuharich, who didn't have a particularly strong tenure as the head coach of the Irish, but who held a 3-1 record over USC.

Maybe John Robinson had it figured out in his two turns as USC coach. He was 6-1 in his first go-round, but just 2-2-1 in his second. "Sometimes things don't always go your way. Coaching can be like that. And when that happens, you become vulnerable. It is part of the business."[55]

There's often a curtain of sorts around sports; they're set off from the real world, a game. Time certainly operates differently, whether in terms of baseball's innings or basketball's timeouts. Being cognizant of the fact that time works in a different way than it normally does opens the door for additional meanings, enjoyments, and lessons.

Another example of sportsmanship outside of Notre Dame can be found at the 2009 College Conference of Illinois and Wisconsin Swimming Championship. After Carthage College men's swimming team completed their meet and was packing to leave, Isaac Rothenbaum noticed Jonathan Nitz, a Wheaton College swimmer, alone in the pool. Rothenbaum discovered that Nitz was about to swim a time trial – with no one in the pool but himself – in an attempt to reach a qualifying time that would be good enough to allow him to compete in nationals.

Recognizing that Nitz could use as much moral support as he could get to hit his mark, , Rothenbaum led his Carthage teammates in cheering him on. Nitz completed the time-trial with a bunch of swimmers screaming him on and managed to qualify for nationals.[56] In addition to being honored as the most outstanding participant in Division III, Rothenbaum was later recognized for his exemplary sportsmanship when the NCAA crowned him 2009 Division III Sportsman of the Year [57]

Examples of this kind of sportsmanship can always be found in other times and places, whether it is in running, sailing, or back in football. We also see it when our coaches and players demonstrate respect for their opponents, the game itself and the opportunity to be part of the game.

The 2014 season didn't go as well for the Irish as it seemed it might. Starting off with winning the first six games and a "should have won" against Florida State, the last half of the season went in the opposite direction. That poor luck affected Irish kicker Kyle Brindza, who struggled in his last season at ND. In the midst of all this adversity, though, he was grateful for being at Notre Dame and part of the team.

"It's a blessing to just be here," he wrote. "I'm excited for the real world and what's to come. But everything I'll have later on in life I'll have learned from here.[58]

Such examples demonstrate that people can play and watch sports and find tremendous meaning and inspiration beyond who wins and losses. Indeed, there are many levels of sports engagement. Do our spirits soar as we join with 100,000 other voices to cheer on our team? Of course. Do we celebrate and feel psychologically rewarded when out team wins? Sure; we might even claim that God was on our side. But we are all affected by these examples of great sportsmanship; they lift our hearts. Unfortunately, sports also has its share of bad and ugly moments.

CHAPTER FOUR

In the Stands:
What We Can Learn as Fans

"Notre Dame sucks and so do you," the orange-clad Longhorn fan blurted as he staggered toward me. The 1978 Cotton Bowl, which would decide the 1977 national championship, was about to begin and the inebriated Texan had wandered into the Irish section attempting to provoke a fight. Fortunately, his behavior was a far cry from that of every other Longhorn fan I had encountered the previous week, as well as with my positive history with Texas.

The week before the Cotton Bowl, I travelled to Austin to hang out with my aunt, a professor at UT, during the winter break of my sophomore year at Notre Dame. The Texas fans could not have been more gracious, even as I wore my ND clothes all over town. When they did needle me, it was in good spirits, such as when the waiter at The Magic Time Machine discovered my Domer-ness and suggested I clear the tables myself while he took my seat. I took him up on the offer. So when the drunk insulted me at the stadium, I chalked it up to an aberration. After the game, I embraced my orange-clad aunt, fully understanding the dignity and decency of the "other side." Sportsmanship can unite opponents very effectively.

I know there have been drunken Irish fans who have replicated the behavior of that Longhorn fan. Indeed, while many will disagree with me, I can pinpoint the time when I found our fans' conduct lousy. It took place eleven years later, when we claimed our 1988 championship.

While Notre Dame's rise from some lean years was dramatic, I always felt that what happened in 1988, when our game with Miami suddenly turned ugly was as misguided as the behavior of the Longhorn fan. Fortunately, there are enough good stories to make me believe that what I saw in 1988 was an aberration for Irish fans, just as that Longhorn drunk was for Texas. Just as we can learn from what we see in the field, we can also learn from what we observe in the stands.

When Notre Dame announced the hiring of Lou Holtz as the new coach of the Irish in 1985, hearts leapt and we knew were back on the road to national prominence. Yet, we still had one game to play to finish the season under the admirable Coach Gerry Faust. The 58-7 mauling Miami put on us to finish the season under Faust was awful, but with Holtz set to assume the reins the following season, revenge awaited. Our 5-6 record? In the rear-view mirror. Scores would be settled against Michigan, Purdue and Penn State. While not on the same level as a traditional rivalry such as Michigan State, everyone knew the test of the resurgence would center on Miami.

Both schools were independents and played each other for several years without producing much of a buzz, since Miami just wasn't at the same level as the Irish. But when Howard Schnellenberg took over Miami's program in 1979, the Hurricanes surged. Jimmy Johnson continued the program's national dominance and he cultivated an aggressive, against-the-rules image that culminated in the 1987 championship game against Joe Paterno's Penn State team when Miami players showed up in military fatigues and brazenly challenged Penn State. This galvanized Irish fans more than the 58-7 whipping.

The Irish did not play the Hurricanes in 1986, Holtz's first year at the helm, but they were an ever-present pole star as the Irish rebuilt with its second consecutive 5-6 season, which had an entirely different feel from the previous year. The Irish were *in* every game, and things finally turned in a dramatic, 17-point, fourth-quarter comeback at USC to end the season and set up the Irish to improve the following year.

Miami beat the Irish 24-0 in 1987, but that was an improvement from the 58-7 drubbing. Fans and players alike took dead-aim at the 1988 game, which had an unbelievable build-up. #1 Miami. #4 Notre Dame. National championship implications. Revenge. Trash talking.

Catholics vs. Convicts.

The first time I saw that tee-shirt, I laughed. The second time, I winced. By the time I taught some Miami players in an Executive MBA Program, I viewed it as an utter embarrassment. Yes, Miami had some guys who had gotten into trouble and the team certainly cultivated a defiant swagger. And yes, there is that halo around ND. But we Domers aren't perfect, just as the folks from Miami weren't villains. It was part of a rivalry that, along with several other incidents got so carried away that ND (rightly) ended the series to let everyone cool off.

But back in October, 1988, the stadium was full a half hour before the game, already rocking in anticipation. There were plenty of spectators around when the fight broke out between the teams in the north end zone, just a few feet from where I was sitting. An already-fired-up crowd went into orbit. There had also been a pre-game altercation before the Michigan game that year a month before. The only time I have seen the Irish crowd that wired pre- game was before the 1977

USC contest with Dan Devine's green jerseys and Trojan horse.

    Before the game, Holtz challenged his team to keep their heads, but if there was a fight later, to leave Jimmy Johnson for him. Even without that additional jolt, the fans never let up during a game filled with great stops, amazing catches, clutch plays and some controversy to boot. There was plenty of material to claim that God had smiled on the Irish yet again as we rode a magical year to the national championship.

    Divine intervention was harder to claim the following year when the teams met again with the one-loss Hurricanes ending the Irish's 23-game winning streak. Miami and the Irish finished with the same record but the head-to-head win, late in the season, tipped the scales in Miami's favor (a logic mysteriously not applied four years later with the Irish and Florida State). But the 1990 Irish win in this new rubber-match within the series allowed the Catholics to trump the Convicts.

    The football team may get most of the headlines, but the basketball team – and its fans – has had its share of the spotlight as well. When I was in school in the late 70s, the basketball program was as prominent as the football team, even though the football team won the national championship. Irish basketball ranked consistently in the top 10 and often higher. The conductor of this Irish excellence was Digger Phelps.

    Memories may dull over time, but in the 1970s, Digger's basketball teams brought some of the most amazing, exciting sports moments to the Dome. Digger made sure the fans were integral to the game. He cultivated the students early on by making trips to the residence halls. That personal touch tapped into student interest and carried over into the basketball arena.

Young and dapper, Digger would saunter out of the tunnel, catching the crowd's attention and bringing the ACC to a roar. He would slowly look around, surveying the increasing tumult. Then he would put his hand behind his ear as if he couldn't hear anyone. Eardrums started to ache at that point and as he continued the conducting, the team burst out of the tunnel and the band kicked into the Victory March.

It was also during those years that the band began to play the 1812 Overture and the students in section 108 began to wave their arms up and down, once so much that the bleachers unhinged from the wall and careened toward the lower seats, where my seats were located. Fortunately, I missed that game because I was studying for an exam.

The basketball team has a way of facing #1 ranked teams and quite often, beating them. Topping the upsets of top-ranked teams, of course, was when ND ended UCLA's 88 game win streak. Undefeated and top-ranked Marquette and DePaul met their downfalls in the ACC during that time as well, and the tradition continued in the 80s with a win over Ralph Sampson-led Virginia.

Yet ND fans have no greater moment than in the 1977 upset of #1 San Francisco. Replacing the traditional cheer of "We Are...ND" with "29...and 1," Irish fans were utterly relentless, keeping the Irish on top of the game and helping to motivate the team to a huge upset over the Bill Cartright-led Dons. I'll never forget when Cartright, who later helped take the Chicago Bulls to three NBA championships, walked up the court late in the game and looked at the crowd in amazement. NBC later gave the student body the MVP award.[59] My fellow students gave me a standing ovation in class the following

Monday when I proved my part in the game by having laryngitis.

In his book, Digger Phelps explains how freshman at the 1974 upset of UCLA were seniors when San Francisco came to town and the freshman for the San Francisco game were seniors when DePaul entered the ACC. That memory, Phelps suggests, helped the crowd remember how to get into an opponent's head. When my senior year came around, I remembered that San Francisco game.

Singing national anthems was something I enjoyed and as a member of the Glee Club, I sang it many times, the most memorable when I sang it as an acappella solo for the Chicago White Sox the day after they clinched the 1983 Division Championship. I had always wanted to play in the majors and was even offered a tryout from the Milwaukee Brewers. While that journey wasn't meant to be, I did stand at home plate as every one of the White Sox was introduced and took his place on the third-base line.

The Glee Club was to sing the Anthem for the game against DePaul, who came into the game #1 and 25-0. Shortly before we went onto the floor, four guys approached me because I was president of the Club. They had taped 25-1 on the backs of their blue blazers so they would be facing the student body when we took the floor to sing.

"Is it OK?" they asked. I was jealous I hadn't thought of it myself. From that San Francisco game three years earlier, I knew exactly what was going to happen. The crowd went crazy and Phelps called it "the all-time spirit stunt."[60]

The game is an experience of life from which players as well as fans can learn and grow. Fans can make a difference in a game. In 1987, the Irish were on the verge of another #1 upset, this time over North Carolina. With a five point lead and seconds to go, though, the fans started throwing placards that had been distributed before the game onto the floor. Digger took to the microphone and told them to stop. They did it again. Then he really let the crowd have it. While players and coaches love to talk about the importance of fans, fans must follow rules and requirements too. Digger may have wanted the fans' passion, but not just anything goes.

Being a fan is not just about yelling your brains out. There's as much to appreciate and learn about being a fan as there is to learn about being a player. One philosopher argues that when we watch an athlete, "we feel as though we ourselves had personally achieved something....the athlete makes all of us be vicariously completed."[61] Fans do sit or stand and observe. They participate too, sometimes in a very visceral way; other times, more above-the-fray.

Moreover, a Notre Dame fan is pretty certain to enjoy other games and absorb meaningful dimensions of a game that doesn't even involve ND. Actually, some of the best lessons might appear when fans aren't cheering for their own team. It's pretty easy to watch one game and flip the channel to the next. In a class I taught, I witnessed how deeply a fan– a professional football player, in fact – could learn from a game he didn't even witness.

In April, 2008, senior Sara Tucholsky, a softball player for Western Oregon University, hit her first home run ever, clearing the center field fence and driving in two runners. She had missed first base on her run, came back to tag it, and collapsed in pain. Under the rules, she couldn't be assisted around the bases by her coach or teammates. So a few players from the opposing team picked her up and carried her around the bases themselves.

An All-Pro NFL defensive end who was a student in my EMBA class took note of this story and used it in a paper as an example of an action that exemplified good. He also confided that when he read the story, he wept. Yep, a 6'5" NFL lineman. That is the kind of impact sports can have on a fan. Players are fans too and learn by watching as well as playing.

Can fans teach each other about good sportsmanship by the way they treat each other in the stands? The difficulty of finding examples of good sportsmanship in the stands tells us more about society as a whole than it does fan sportsmanship itself. Good sportsmanship makes for a dull news story, while stupidity gets ink. Passion for a team is great, but fans cross lines when they threaten the physical well-being of opponents and accost opposing players as if they were rats. It's not hard to find examples of fans and players brawling in the stands, throwing objects or taunting players – even issuing death threats.

Television and the media gravitate to conflicts (and sex). It's easy, interesting and titillating to capture a fight on screen. There is a remarkable preponderance of fan fights, hockey fights, youth gang brawls and seemingly thousands of WWE events on YouTube. While it may be true that sports provide a channeled way to combat, the videos are hard to balance with something as bland as good sportsmanship.

What fan hasn't been in a stadium and embarrassed by a foul-mouthed drunk spewing garbage, often near children? Even websites devoted to promoting good sportsmanship spend the bulk of their space decrying poor sportsmanship instead. As a result, a lot of good behavior goes unrecognized, whether one is sitting in the stands in Ann Arbor, Austin and certainly in South Bend.

November 13, 1993 marked one of the best moments of my Notre Dame fan career. The #1 ranked Florida State Seminoles, led by Coach Bobby Bowden and Heisman Trophy Winner Charley Ward, came into the stadium of #2 ranked Notre Dame. The Irish dominated throughout, but it was still a dramatic game, ending with a knocked-down pass with less than a minute to go to thwart a tying Florida State touchdown and preserve the Notre Dame win.

I loved that game and its excitement, but my favorite part was sitting behind two Florida State fans. In the midst of our alternating cheering, we struck up a conversation. They told me they followed the Seminoles all over the country and had never been treated with such hospitality and a sense of welcome as they had that day. Domers had said hello, helped with directions, were unfailingly polite and gracious and welcomed them to Notre Dame. I don't want to put the halo on my alma mater; I've seen my share of lousy behavior. Domer hospitality, however, is not a one-off.

In a long Internet post, a BYU fan praised ND hospitality in great detail. After sitting in the stands he wrote:

> This experience made me a Notre Dame fan. As fans of Utah schools, I think we can learn something from the Notre Dame fan base. We have a good fan base that is educated enough to rival a Notre Dame fan base. They proved that we can keep

our passion for the game but welcome visitors to our stadium. If we want people to return to Utah for more games, we need to start following Notre Dame's example. I have never welcomed a fan to Rice Eccles or LaVell Edwards Stadium, but I will start. Notre Dame fans cheered just as loudly as fans at a BYU vs. Utah game, but in the end I felt welcome and am grateful for the experience.[62]

Some scholars argue that *basking in reflected glory* (BIRG) refers to an individual's inclination to "share in the glory of a successful other with whom they are in some way associated."[63] We see this all the time. When your favorite team is winning, it suddenly has more fans proudly claiming their affiliation.

When I was at Notre Dame, my singing group toured the country each year. If the football team had a good season, we had no problem finding organizations that wanted to host a concert. However if the football team had a tough year, it was also tougher for us to get a full slate of concerts. I doubt our popularity or lack of had anything to do with critics' reviews; more likely, fans wanted to BIRG in those winning seasons.[64] In bad years, people needed to find reasons other than BIRG to hear us sing.

Win or lose, though, one can be moved by a game – and by the fans – even if one isn't experiencing BIRG. That was true with the BYU and Florida fans. We see another example, this time between the Boston Celtics and the Los Angeles Lakers – perhaps the bitterest, most long-standing, consequential rivalry in the NBA. Sometimes, the rivalry has lead to bad fan behavior. But after the Celtics beat the Lakers in the 2008 NBA finals, a blogger wrote:

> I have a very bittersweet taste in my mouth (mostly very bitter). I am extremely depressed that the Lakers have lost and that the 2008 season is over. Another trip to the NBA Finals two wins short of a championship and nothing to show for it, besides pride of making it so far of course. I am very upset right now and don't even want to think about basketball.
>
> With that said, I'd like to congratulate the Boston Celtics franchise, but more importantly Kevin Garnett, Paul Pierce, and Ray Allen. There have been times that us Lakers fans have made fun of them ... but the bottom line is that they have heart. The end of this series is enough evidence of how badly KG and the boys wanted this title. It means the world to them and I'm very happy for them that they have finally achieved what they wanted for so long.
>
> There is only one champion, and this year, the Boston Celtics are the NBA Champions. Congratulations!

Who says being a sports fan can't be inspiring?

Awareness of various dimensions of the game can help diffuse a situation that might get out of hand. At the end of the 1980 football season that saw Harry Oliver's dramatic field goal win the Michigan game, Notre Dame played in the Sugar Bowl against the University of

Georgia, led by the sensational freshman Herschel Walker. In 1980, bowl bids came out in November and weren't based on computer ratings but rather on polls and reputation, with conference champions committed to specific bowls: The Big 8 champion played in the Orange Bowl, the Southwest Conference champion played in the Cotton Bowl and the champions from the Big Ten and Pac 8 played in the Rose Bowl. The Southeast Conference champion played in the Sugar Bowl.

At the time the pairing with Notre Dame was set, it looked like it might be a game for the national championship, but a shocking late season tie (3-3) with Georgia Tech, followed by a heartbreaking loss in Los Angeles to USC sent the Irish into the Sugar Bowl with a 9-1-1 record that eliminated any title hopes.

Undefeated Georgia was #1 but it had been awhile since Georgia had been in title contention. Its fans were enthusiastic as they cruised the French Quarter in New Orleans on New Year's Eve. Not surprisingly, most folks that night were a little tipsy and the shouting between the Georgia and Notre Dame fans seemed inevitable. Initially fun, it soon edged toward hostile. I strode straight over to a Bulldog fan, aware he might slug me preemptively, stuck out my hand and said, "Herschel Walker is one helluva player. I hope we beat you guys, but it will be tough with a stud like that."

The guy stepped back, then shook my hand and drunkenly agreed that Walker was just about the second coming of Christ. He then started to talk about how exciting the game was going to be, what a great match-up it was and how cool it was to play ND etc, etc. etc. The mood changed and the fans from both sides mixed it up happily after that. None of us left our passion for our team behind. We just recognized the other side was good too. The "as good as it gets" dimension changed the dynamic that night in one block of the French Quarter.

You usually have a choice about how to behave. Evidence shows that ethical business behavior is weakly correlated with financial performance: being ethical in business doesn't always pay and being crummy in business doesn't always cost. But people are not forced to be jerks nor are they forced to be ethical in order to succeed. You can be successful either way. The advantage of choosing the more spiritual dimensions of sports is that they are fun and don't mean you have to abandon enthusiasm for your own team.

There are times when even the most rabid fans will stop to recognize something beyond their passion for their team. Opening ceremonies, particularly in times of crisis during the National Anthem, counteract some of the venom associated with *us vs. them* fandom. Rituals remind fans that beyond their teams' victories is a larger world to which we pay allegiance and which impacts us. Singing the National Anthem right after the terrorist attacks of September 11, 2001 enables us to transcend.

Even outside a crisis, games are filled with ceremony; shaking of hands, singing the anthem, standing at attention. When set within a secular event, there is still a religious aura to the framing of a game.[65] That may be just another form of *us vs. them* - i.e. our country against an enemy, but such moments still provide access to wider, richer and more colorful forms of spirituality.

Respect for the rules is a step beyond *us vs. them* because you really can't have a raucous rivalry without some rules and regulations. You might not even have a rivalry because without rules, what would fans argue about? Fans of the Denver Broncos and Cleveland

Browns, bitter NFL playoff rivals in the 1980s, have no other reason to hate each other than because of their respective quests to get to the Super Bowl. While fans from New York and Boston might find other reasons to detest each other, some rivalries only exist because of the rules that allow games to be played and championships to be won. Some of these rules are the stuff of officiating, but not all of them are.

It takes rules to create a tournament. How else could we figure out what teams would be in the World Series? It's only when regulations passed by an organization like the NCAA or Major League Baseball determine division or conference winners and wild card teams does an after-season event occur. A team only gets to keep playing when they triumph in a winner-take-all game or a majority of games in a series. These are rules that pre-exist offside and balk calls.

Other kinds of rules are more informal, which does not mean unimportant. They relate to routines – including superstitions – that players and fans alike follow in order to try to tip the forces of the universe toward their team's favor.

Sports are filled with rituals. They are essential to a game. I like to get to a football game about an hour early to watch punting practice just as I like to get to a baseball game early to watch batting practice. The early-bird in me certainly wants to soak up as much of the day as I can, but there is more to it than that. I love to watch the rituals of the sport because they ask us to prepare for the game itself, not just yell for our own team.

Until 2015, the Band of the Fighting Irish hadn't changed the pre-game routine much in fifty years. (Unfortunately, TV pressure forced the band to truncate the pre-game show starting in 2015.) My kids are very impressed when I narrate exactly what is going to happen next. "How do you know that Dad?" they ask.

The band comes charging out of the tunnel, spreading out onto the field. As the announcer introduces them amidst truncated phrases from the Victory March, they spring into the famous hike step while playing "Hike Notre Dame." They salute the visiting team with a rather tame version of the school song and then spell out *Irish* as they play the greatest of all college songs, *The Notre Dame Victory March*. Then it is into *America the Beautiful* and finally, the *National Anthem*, nearly always conducted by the director of the visiting school's band. You can set your clock by this ritual.

Other sports, schools and events have their own rituals that we get to enjoy as visiting fans. Even aside from championship games, teams play for a trophy such as "The Little Brown Jug" that goes to the winner of the annual Minnesota-Michigan game. Baseball stops for a 7th inning stretch; sometimes with a rendition of *Take Me out to the Ballgame*. Other sports fill halftimes with entertainment. The list goes on and on. We love these rituals and they deepen our love of the game. With our superstitions, we can believe that wearing of the same unwashed underwear during the nine-game winning streak really might keep the forces of the universe aligned with our teams' success. Well, maybe we don't, but we love that part of our engagement with the game.

Why do fans partake in all these rituals? Many will go to a game dressed in the team's colors; that unity might actually help the team. But fans also wear the team's colors when they're sitting on the couch, still believing it will have an impact on the game. I have heard more than a few fans insist that the lucky jersey they wear two thousand miles away from the game is the key to success. Spill some onion dip on the jersey and take it off and boom! The other team goes on a 15-0 run. Clearly, the jersey did it. I've even known a few fans who not only believed their underwear was the lucky charm, but that the *sequence* of underwear – one particular pair per quarter – was the reason the team won or lost.

There may be some psychological issues with the serial underpants changer, but I doubt if a slightly less-extreme behavior is all that unusual. These fans feel spiritually connected to their teams and believe they may be able to influence the outcome of the game from afar.

As fans, we can even relish a game beyond enjoying the atmosphere of a great fall afternoon between rivals. We can place the meaning of fandom into a much larger metaphysical context. For example, at least prior to 2016, Sisyphus would have been a Cubs fan. In ancient Greek mythology, he constantly pushed a rock up the side of a mountain, but when it got close to the top, it would roll back to the bottom, where he resumed pushing. To the Greeks, never attaining the ultimate goal or peak was a horrible existence.

Albert Camus, the French philosopher, disagreed. Even without attaining the ultimate goal, Camus believed people could find great meaning and satisfaction in the day-to-day stuff that makes up a typical life.

My parents married in 1945, the last year the Chicago Cubs were in the World Series. They lost in six games to the Detroit Tigers. My father, a life-long Cubs fan, assured my mother, a willing-to-learn wife, that there was nothing to worry about. The Cubs were so good that they would be in the Series every three or four years. It was just a matter of time before they returned to the Series and were triumphant. Forty-eight years later my mother died and five years after that, a full fifty-three years since that 1945 appearance, my father went to his grave still waiting. In fact, the Chicago Cubs went 100 years before winning a World Series.

Cubs' fans don't cheer for the Cubs because the rock of a World Series reaches the top of Sisyphus' mountain. That would be grand, but Cubs fans have a greater existential appreciation of the joys of baseball. There is a joy of a game under the sun at Wrigley Field. There is the fun of the annual blossoming of hope and moments of triumph. There are the memories of characters who extend beyond the field to the press box, seen in icons such as Harry Carey or Jack Brickhouse.

As a Cubs fan for fifty years myself, I cried when the Cubs won the World Series in 2016. My sister texted me seconds later. It had little to do with the joy of our team winning; rather, it had to do with memories of our parents' decades of disappointment. It had to do with my niece writing my father's name on the Wrigley Field wall and the fellow who listened to the World Series games at his father's grave. It had to do with what went into pushing the rock up the hill.

When the Cubs won, a lot of fans – at least the ones I knew – reflected on the place of a hundred-year championship famine and what that meant in their families and lives. Indeed, it will be interesting to see what happens with Cubs fans now that they have won because that unique sports struggle will be much different.... unless the Cubs go another hundred years until the next World Series win!

The Cubs are not the only team with a woebegone history. The Boston Red Sox and Chicago White Sox endured decades-long championship droughts. The Cleveland Indians would have been everyone's sentimental favorite in 2016 because of their 50 year drought had they not been playing the Cubs. Navy went 43 years between wins against Notre Dame. Those championships and wins were sweet for the teams and their fans and rightly cherished. In a strange way, the fans also cherished the suffering.

Being a fan of a struggling team can be good preparation for struggles in city hall, business, church or the neighborhood school. Will your ethical actions transform the moral character of that organization? Maybe and maybe not. You may not get to the top of that mountain, but being ethical for its own sake and for your own self can still be rewarding…just like cheering for the Cubs.

Growing up in Illinois, I cheered for Chicago sports teams and they taught me some great lessons. When I started first grade, my parents told my teacher they weren't sure if I knew my alphabet, but I could recite the starting line-up and jersey numbers for the Chicago Bears, who had just won the 1963 NFL Championship. Being from west central Illinois, I didn't have to choose sides in the rivalry between the Cubs and the White Sox as you do if you are from Chicago; I cheered for both. I followed the Bulls and Blackhawks in the daily sports pages of *The Chicago Tribune* and regional radio stations, WGN, WMAQ, and WBBM. During all these years of Chicago fandom, I've never seen anyone quite like Michael Jordan.

Jordan was spectacular from the start of his career. Fantastic shots, prolific scoring, nightly ESPN highlights. The Bulls weren't championship material, though, until Jordan combined his singular, clutch-playmaking ability with a willingness to give up the shot to a teammate with a better one. The Bulls won their first championship over the Los Angeles Lakers when, down the stretch in the deciding game, Jordan consistently drew the Lakers toward him and dished the ball off to John Paxson (from Notre Dame, of course) who drained shot after shot. Jordan's maturity in fostering teamwork is so obvious we sometimes forget its significance. It was a lesson of the benefits of unselfishness and how it made for a successful – a championship – team.

The fun thing – and the rich thing – about being a fan is that there are so many ways to enjoy a game. We can love winning of course, especially when hammering a bitter rival. We can relish seeing a game that is *as good as it gets* and features adherence to rules and discipline, which make the game more meaningful. The Super Bowl isn't just about the two best teams playing a game; it is its own cultural phenomena that fans relish. In a similar way, March Madness becomes its own event to behold.

Moreover, sportsmanship hardly lessens our passion; indeed, it makes it richer because fans know there is more than a game to savor, regardless of whether their team wins or not. Respect for the other team and its fans leads to a love of the game, where the tee-shirts before the game don't say, "to hell with the other team," but instead place both teams on the shirt with "As Good As It Gets."

As the opening of this book shows, fans can sometimes become violent with each other. It might be a dramatic TV image to see opposing fans yelling at each other even if they aren't fighting. Yet fans can mingle with each other quite amiably, even while good-naturedly needling each other. One of the unique things I have found in over thirty-five years of my Notre Dame affiliation is that while our biggest rival is the University of Southern California, the fans of both schools seem to like each other. I can remember many occasions of partying with the SC fans before and after a game and while each side took victory and defeat seriously, there was something of an affection between the two sides. I can even empathize with a "hated" figure from USC if I think he's been badly treated.

I didn't cheer for Lane Kiffin or his decision to leave the University of Tennessee and return to USC in January, 2010. I remembered too well how his offenses destroyed us for years during the Pete Carroll era. But after five hundred fans set fire to a mattress to protest and Internet message boards wished him and his wife personal harm, Kiffin had to be given protection by the Knox County police. All this occurred during the horror of the earthquake in Haiti. Much as one might disparage Kiffin, all perspective went out the window, as it did when Tennessee won the recruiting battle for Peyton Manning. Manning's family received hate mail from fans angry he chose not to follow his father's footsteps to Ole Miss. Stuff like this is nuts.

There's a fairly significant field of study of sports sociology and psychology that spends its time looking at reactions like these. There is no one theory of sports sociology of course, but the research some scholars have conducted sheds light on the existential reasons why fans get a bit too serious about their teams and their teams' opponents.

Sports sociologist Daniel Wann suggests that being a fan supplies eight different psychological needs: *eustress*, a kind of happiness-producing stress that results from achieving positive gains, self-esteem benefits, escape from everyday life, entertainment, economic factors (gambling), aesthetic (artistic) qualities, group affiliation and family needs.[66] No one person may watch sports and fulfill all of them. But clearly there are multiple aspects of personal identity and happiness that comprise these needs, which were previously filled by our mediating institutions: our neighborhoods, religious organizations, and bowling clubs, for example. The idea that we watch sports to satisfy some of these needs suggests we aren't able to do so elsewhere, or at least not very well.

Other scholars argue that contemporary society has become bereft of those mediating institutions – the Stronghursts of the world – that taught me, via my sister, not to boo at the basketball game. What has replaced them? Sports. One scholar argues that "…sports spectating has emerged as a major urban structure where spectators come together not only to be entertained but to enrich their social-psychological lives through the sociable, quasi-intimate relationships available."[67]

In short, there is a lot at stake in being a fan. Individual psychological fulfillment, sociological identity. If a team goes sour, much of a person's self-image could be impacted. You can see why fans sometimes get carried away with the atmosphere and emotions of a game.

On the field, taunting may bring a fifteen yard penalty for unsportsmanlike conduct. The rules in the stands, however, are a good deal more lax. Short of shaming by other fans, punching an abusive fan in the mouth, or someone getting so carried away that security has to be summoned, there is no external discipline that can be enforced against a fan. It's either self-discipline or vigilantism.

So what does being a fan mean? "The primary difference between the sports fan and the non-fan," one scholar notes, "is that the fan accepts the illusion that the result of the contest matters, while the non-fan is indifferent to the result"[68] Fair enough, but a lot of people take things far more seriously.

According to some sources, "fan" comes from the Latin *fanum,* meaning "the sacred, the beneficial, the salvific, the temple, the consecrated place." *Webster's Sports Dictionary* (1976) sees *fan* growing from *fanatic* out of the Latin *fanaticus,* meaning frenzied. Others note that "the term *fanatic* was used in Latin literature and referred to being put into an intensely enthusiastic state by a deity." [69]

Being a fan plays upon some deep psychological needs and in attempting to find fulfillment, identity and meaning, those deep urges reach for deep resources. Connect the two and deep enthusiasm results. You might even become so spirited about the connection that you become fanatical. To maintain your status as a fan often requires some self-sacrifice to remain a member of the team. That doesn't have to be scary or dark.

Just as players can exhibit admirable sportsmanship, so too can fans. Football teams travelling to Morgantown, WV to take on the West Virginia Mountaineers can often expect to be greeted not only by a formidable opponent, but also by a rabid, loud and oft-crass fan base. Insults are hurled at the players, crowd noise alters offensive game plans, and WVU students typically burn couches after games to celebrate home victories.

In October 2009, however, the Mountaineer faithful took a temporary turn toward civility. The reason? UConn's starting cornerback and talented return man Jasper Howard had been murdered the week before and the Huskies were emotionally spent before encountering their first blue-and-gold-clad fanatic.

The West Virginia fan base was in fact *very* supportive of the visiting Huskies, cheering them on as they emerged from the tunnel before the game. Many fans held signs of support; the fans who on any other week might have been quick to swear or yell at a visiting team were, for this game at least, even quicker to show the Huskies some compassion, chanting "Jasper Howard" in the moments before the game.

"The sportsmanship and the love and the concern that they showed for our team, I don't know if you've ever seen that in sports," said UConn head coach Randy Edsall. "My hat is off to them. They're a bunch of class fans, and it's a class coaching staff and administration, and I would just like to say thank you to them."[70]

A moment of silence was held before the opening kick. Then the teams did their best to return to normalcy. West Virginia won, 28-24, with the support of their lively – though civil – fans.

"I'm so proud to be a West Virginian today," Mountaineers head coach Bill Stewart said.[71]

Another example of exceptional compassion and sportsmanship occurred after Virginia Tech was terrorized by the bloodiest school shooting in American history.[72] A morning shooting spree began at a dormitory and ended in a classroom building, leaving thirty-three dead, including the gunman, a Virginia Tech senior suffering from a severe anxiety disorder.[73] The news of Cho's previous violent tendencies and the school's immediate response to the event shocked students, parents, and the nation, sparking the insistence that higher education communities establish emergency preparedness and notification plans. The event also inspired tens of thousands of students to band together and show support for the Virginia Tech community.

At Penn State just a few days later, 71,000 fans turned out for the football team's annual Blue-White spring intra-squad game. Instead of donning their usual blue and white Penn State apparel, thousands of the Nittany Lion faithful arrived at the game wearing maroon and orange, the signature colors of the Virginia Tech Hokies. After a moment of silence at the start of the day, the Penn State cheerleaders led a chant of "Let's go, Hokies," followed by a musical salute from the Penn State Blue Band, which was also in maroon and orange. Even the "S" made up of students in the senior section of Beaver Stadium was scrapped in favor of a maroon and orange "VT" using 800 Hokie-colored tee-shirts.

These stories inspire us, as well they should. It was Aristotle who suggested that most of our ethical actions are so engrained in our nature, they are simply part of our character. With that in mind, consider the Louisville fan, who travelling to South Bend to see her Cardinals upset the Irish, wrote:

> The quote of the day came from a Notre Dame fan when he turned to our Louisville friend, with whom he had been chatting prior to the game, and said "I hope you lose, but I also hope you have a really good time today." That summed up the entire mentality of all the Notre Dame fans. Friendly, fun, and great sportsmen. The fact that they didn't win but acted like winners is the greatest lesson we can learn from them.[74]

CHAPTER FIVE

In the Stadium and Beyond

Businesses have often been called upon to battle injustice; sometimes that injustice is connected with peace; other times not. I teach issues of ethics in business and how ethical business behavior can contribute to peace in the world. If that sounds like a lot of things that might be talked about at Notre Dame, it shows I learned my lessons well. In my academic career, I have often said, "I'm a Notre Dame guy doing Notre Dame stuff; I'm just not doing it at Notre Dame."

When I was in college, Father Ollie Williams demonstrated the connections between business and peace with his work in apartheid South Africa. There were some case studies about the relationship between the two, but not a great deal of theoretical work, which I began to examine in 1999. Others did as well, and we held a major conference at Notre Dame in November, 2006.

The night before the conference, our hosts – Father Williams and the amazing Lee Tavis – held a dinner in a reception area located just behind the press box in the stadium. The participants were going to have dinner and be entertained by the Glee Club followed by a speaker. As a former Clubber, I was invited to join the group on stage for the final songs.

My family had driven to South Bend earlier in the day from Washington, DC, where I was teaching at

George Washington University. I had promised my six year old I would get back to the hotel to give her a good night kiss, so I would have to leave shortly after the speaker began.

I didn't want to interrupt the speech but unfortunately the elevator opened to a space in the midst of the audience. It would be very disruptive for me to get up, ring for the elevator and leave while the speaker was talking. There had to be a better option.

During dinner, I scoped a way out via the emergency exit stairs. Shortly after the speaker began, I made my exit, ran down several flights of stairs and found the exit door on the ground floor. It seemed like the door should be to my left rather than my right, but I figured I had lost my bearings going around the circles necessary to walk down the stairs. I burst through the exit door and froze. The door slammed behind me. This wasn't right. I reached to pull the door open.

It was locked. Why exit *in* to the stadium rather than *out* of it? Thinking that question was of no help.

Like most alumni my age, I had been in Notre Dame Stadium dozens of times, so I knew where to find the nearest gates. They were locked too. Initially, I just felt annoyed. Then, I thought: *This is awesome! I have the entire stadium to myself!*

I walked out to the seats to see if I really was all by myself. I didn't see a soul. I could see the lights from the press box and a few people whose backs were against the wall, but they were oblivious to me. Even if they had looked into the stadium, I doubt they could have seen me. If anyone else was around, they weren't anywhere nearby, so for all intents and purposes, I really did have the stadium to myself.

I had never considered going out for the football team. It would have been utter madness, if not downright suicidal. I played well-enough in high school, making the all-conference team and setting some state receiving records, but I went to a small school. What's more, my 5'8" frame came out on the losing end of nearly every collision. When I went back to my hometown for a visit, several folks asked me if I had tried for the team. They had no idea of the quantum difference between the level I had played and that of Notre Dame.

So while I had no memories as a player, I sure had great memories as a fan of Notre Dame football. Even more importantly, Notre Dame had taken a farm kid and turned him into a thinker, setting him on his way so he could return to campus as a scholar who had made a name for himself and was now trying to create an academic movement that quested for peace. I believed attempting to contribute to peace was a worthwhile project, even if I failed. While I may have had ambitions growing up, Notre Dame shaped the *aim* of those ambitions.

The Stadium didn't provide this transformative growth for me, but it serves as a metaphor for the university's impact on my life. And given the prominence of the team, what happens at ND Stadium serves as a touchstone for fellow Domers, an icebreaker at reunions. I had experienced many of my most aspirational thoughts at the Grotto – my favorite place on campus – but while the Grotto connected my Notre Dame experience (and me) to God, the Stadium connected my Notre Dame experience (and me) to the world. It was a precious few minutes.

As appreciative as Father Hesburgh might have been about my reflection, I don't think he would have approved of leaving my daughter at the hotel without her nightly kiss. I realized I had to get out. I made a couple of calls from my cell phone to figure out who could help. The woman at campus security chuckled when she heard my story.

"Doesn't happen very often, but it does occur from time to time." She told me where to meet a security officer, but said it would be a half-hour before someone arrived.

I don't care if you are the CEO of a Fortune 100 company, a student, a farmer or anyone else: having Notre Dame Stadium to yourself for thirty minutes is damn cool.

***

"This is Officer Tim McCarthy with the Indiana State Police."

For 55 years, Sergeant Tim McCarthy introduced himself to the fans at Notre Dame Stadium, usually in the fourth quarter. Unless the opposing band, unaware of this peculiar tradition, trampled on McCarthy's introduction, the entire stadium fell utterly silent. Even in the midst of a raucous game, fans stopped whatever they were doing to hear a reminder about traffic safety on the drive home, punctuated with awful puns: "Remember, you won't be taken to the cleaners if your driving is spotless." Or "Your drive home will be heavenly if you drive like an angel."[75]

From his perch in the press box, McCarthy could, of course, look down on the field. But he could also use his perch to see other things, such as the time he noticed some youths breaking into a car. McCarthy alerted a photographer from the South Bend Tribune, who took a picture that was later used by the police to apprehend the perpetrators.[76]

We, too, can shift our vision from the stadium to the outside world. When we do, we can transfer what we learn from one place to the other.

Sports terms and metaphors from sports saturate our public dialogue, sometimes to the great chagrin of our audience. Politics, business and teaching frequently attempt to link lessons from sports to other parts of our lives. When we see the lessons from the Blimp, we transfer what we see in the stadium to what happens beyond it. We see what happens in the stadium and see the application of truths like discipline, honor, fairness and many other virtues to city hall, local business, the classroom and the church. It's almost impossible not to hear people make the connection between sports and daily life for better or worse.

Sports metaphors abound in politics, with their use starting at the top, with Presidents. During a fifty minute question and answer period during the health care reform debate, President Obama used football analogies four times, including this one:

> [I]f I fumble the ball, you know, I'm going to wait until I get the next play, and then I'm going to try to run as hard as I can and do right by the team. So, you know, ultimately I'm the head of this team. We did fumble the ball on it. And what I'm going to do is make sure that we get that fixed.[77]

On another occasion, Obama dismissed opponent Mitt Romney's plan as something that should be "punted away," and once claimed that his health care plan's success was "on the five yard line" and also "in the red zone."[78] Obama's predecessor, George W. Bush, once warned his opponents against "dancing in the end zone" and celebrating an election win too soon."[79] Discussing the violence in Kosovo, Bill Clinton once warned that success in the fight was not "a slam dunk."[80]

Presidential candidates have been bashed with metaphors as well. In an address to the Democratic Convention, Governor Ted Strickland said, "You know, it was once said of the first George Bush that he was born on third base and thought he'd hit a triple. Well, with the 22 million new jobs and the budget surplus Bill Clinton left behind, George W. Bush came into office on third base – then he stole second. And John McCain cheered him every step of the way."[81]

Alaskan Governor Sarah Palin jumped into the game, so to speak, when she said:

> Let me go back to a comfortable analogy for me - sports... basketball. I use it because you're naïve if you don't see the national full-court press picking away right now: A good point guard drives through a full court press, protecting the ball, keeping her eye on the basket... and she knows exactly when to pass the ball so that the team can WIN. And I'm doing that - keeping our eye on the ball that represents sound priorities - smaller government, energy independence, national security, freedom! And I know when it's time to pass the ball - for victory.[82]

Supreme Court justices can jump right in as well. Justice John Roberts told the Senate Judiciary Committee, "Justices and judges are servants of the law, not the other way around. Judges are like umpires. Umpires don't make the rules; they apply them. Nobody ever went to a ballgame to see the umpire."[83]

When Ronald Reagan gave his speech to the 1988 Republican National Convention, he couldn't resist asking the newly-nominated George H.W. Bush to "win one for the old Gipper." Reagan's reach into ND history arose out of his film portrayal of the "Gipper" a ND player who died at twenty-five of a streptococcal throat infection days after he helped beat Northwestern.

I often wonder if in addition to Ara Parseghian's impact, Reagan's portrayal of Knute Rockne slowly changed me from cheering against Notre Dame to cheering for it. I actually met Reagan when I was eleven years old, right before I first cheered for Texas to beat Notre Dame. In 1969, my family took the train from Illinois to California for my cousin Grady's wedding. After we arrived, we attended a staff party for the new Governor because one of my aunts was in the new Governor's secretarial pool. As we entered the party, Reagan had just gone inside to change his clothes after jumping into the swimming pool to rescue a child.[84] When he returned, we had our photo taken with him and learned he was raised in Western (and Northern) Illinois. We later snuck into his office, sat at his desk and stole some of his jellybeans. He almost caught us after he came in up the private elevator with one of the Apollo 9 astronauts.

People use sports idioms all the time and may not even be aware the expressions stem from sports. Some of the more famous sayings come from Notre Dame.

Though often attributed to Joseph P. Kennedy, Frank Leahy actually said, "When the going gets tough, the tough get going." [85] Leahy was certainly following the lead of his mentor, Knute Rockne, who gave us the following gems:

- Show me a good loser, and I'll show you a loser

- One man practicing sportsmanship is far better than a hundred teaching it.

- Build up your weaknesses until they become your strong points

- Win or lose, do it fairly.

- One loss is good for the soul. Too many losses is not good for the coach.

- The secret is to work less as individuals and more as a team. As a coach, I play not my eleven best, but my best eleven.

- Winning too often is as disastrous as losing too often. Both get the same results, the falling off of the public's enthusiasm.

- I have found that prayers work best when you have big players [86]

Rockne's successors have continued the tradition. Who hasn't heard Ara Parseghian's famous quote or something close to it, "We have no breaking point," Lou

Holtz's "You'll never get ahead of anyone as long as you try to get even with him." Joe Montana joins in as well with, "If you don't want to be the best then there's no reason going out and trying to accomplish anything."[87]

Whether in business, politics, church, or just about anywhere else, someone's always talking about a *kickoff* event, *staying on target, knowing the ropes, jumping the gun, providing a ballpark figure, having the ball in one's court,* or *being sure not to take your eye off the ball.* There are certainly many idioms from beyond sports that admonish us to *stay in tune* or *keep a stiff upper lip,* but sports phrases are always relevant to our daily life. They are lessons from the blimp, which shows us how the lessons on the field apply to what we see in the courthouse, the workplace or the classroom.

<u>Some Sports Idioms</u>[88]

    Across the board
    Arrow in one's quiver
    At this stage of the game
    Back the wrong horse
    Bat a thousand
    Beat the gun
    Behind the eight ball
    Beyond one's depth
    Blow the whistle
    Blow by blow description
    Bounce something off someone
    Call the shots
    Carry the ball
    Choose sides
    Clear a hurdle
    Come in a close second
    Come out of left field

Cover one's bases
Be Cricket
Dive in headfirst
Dive into something
Doubleheader
Down for the count
Down to the wire
Draw first blood
Drop the ball
Fighting chance
First string
Game Plan
Get one's feet wet
Get off to a fast start
Get the ball rolling
Get to first base
Go a few rounds
Go to bat for
Grand slam
Hand the baton
Hard to call
Have the inside track
Have two/three strikes against you
Hit a home run
Hit a hole in one
Hit a bullseye
Home free
In deep water
In full swing
In someone's corner
In the ballpark
In the bullpen
In the homestretch
In the running
In the same league
Jockey for position
Jump off the deep end
Jump the gun

Keep one's eye on the ball
Know the score
Left at the gate
Level playing field
Make the cut
Miss the cut
Meet one's match
Off and running
Off base
On an even keel
On deck
On side
On the ropes
On your marks
Out of bounds
Paddle one's own canoe
Pinch hit
Pitch an idea
Pitch a curve
Play ball
Play by the rules
Play hardball
Put in one's oar
Rally round
Rest on one's oars
Right off the bat
Root for
Run Interference
Run With
Safe bet
Score points
Send someone to the showers
Set the pace
Sink or Swim
Smooth sailing
Sporting Chance
Steal a base
Step up to the plate

Sticky Wicket
Strike out
Tackle a problem
Take the checkered flag
Take the wind out of one's sales
Test the water
That's the way the ball bounces
Throw in the towel
Thrust and Parry
Toe the line
Too close to call
Touch base
Warm the bench
Whole new ballgame
Wild card
Win by a neck
Win by a nose[89]

Notre Dame, of course, has embraced the message of sports and promotes *what would you fight for* messages during game-time television ads. Some of those messages encourage building better bridges and homes, helping the sick, creating equal opportunity, fostering peace and exploring our universe.[90] The commercials feature the work of students and faculty who use their knowledge and energy to fight for a better world because "We are the Fighting Irish."[91]

Three stories try to account for that name. One account claims that it was used as something of an epithet by Northwestern students, laughing at the play (and perhaps the sobriety) of a bunch of fighting Irishmen in an early Notre Dame football game.[92] Others believe the name stems from the Michigan game – as a challenge to the team; looking at the heritage of the players, they needed to become fighting Irishmen.[93] A third story states that the term originated by Irish who boxed for money in the streets of South Bend in the late 1800s.[94]

Not only does "Fighting Irish" denote our teams; it represents a challenge for ND graduates and what they will achieve with their Notre Dame degree. What will you fight for to make the world better? The great Irish phrase, "Play Like a Champion" has also been used to challenge Domers in their daily work. Holtz brought it to Notre Dame, though it may have originated with Oklahoma. My wife's gift that encourages me to "Teach Like a Champion" is but one of many variations. I may cheer for the team to play like a champion, but then it is on me to do the same when I go onto my field of play: the classroom.

In one of the more elaborate comparisons, Kansas Senator Sam Brownback said:

> ...the most important issue for me is rebuilding the family and renewing the culture. That may seem a little out of step, but...it's like you've got a football team that's got a great quarterback, great defense, great running back on and no line. And so you're looking at it and you're always saying, 'we've gotta have our quarterback performing and he's not performing so well.' Why isn't he? Well, he doesn't have any time to throw the ball. You gotta build the line.[95]

Of course, business is replete with sports metaphors. Red Wilson, former chairman of Nortel Networks, said of his findings as head of a competition (trade) panel: "We must skate harder, shoot harder and keep our elbows up in the corners ..."[96] Former Mets and Phillies player Lenny Dystrka used baseball to teach life lessons in his business:

The one-one count is one baseball metaphors for life, meant to illustrate that some moments, and the choices they bring, are more fateful than others (i.e., the next pitch makes all the difference), or, in this case, that circumstances set in motion during the early stages of development are difficult to overcome later on. If a batter falls behind, one ball and two strikes, he's in a hole from which, the statistics augur, he will not recover, even if he is Barry Bonds; and if he gets ahead, to two balls and one strike, he wrests control from the pitcher and takes charge of his own destiny. Having two parents puts you in control of life's count, and enables you to become a .300 hitter.[97]

I try to go easy on sports metaphors when I am teaching, but it is clear from student comments that I fail. While many students like the metaphors and relate to them, others get weary of what they perceive to be ongoing *sportsification* of life.

That may explain the ideas in a novel written by Bob Katz, *Third and Long*. In the book, the hero is a former Notre Dame football player who takes over a struggling company. At first, he has the employees watch a Lou Holtz video because the company is doing too poorly to afford to bring Lou in person. Holtz is a master of using sports motivations in the business world. After watching his video, the workers are so moved they say they would never bet against ND.

Unfortunately, the workers don't take Holtz's wisdom on teamwork, persistence, guts and faith to heart in their own work, so the company continues to lag. The stakeholders ask the hero/former ND player to inspire and appeal to motivational devices, but he refuses, believing the situation too grim to be equated to a game.[98]

We can overdo sports analogies and diminish what we do by thinking it's game-like. Then again, "games" are often serious all on their own. I'm not talking about the games in which parents get so enmeshed they abuse umpires and get violent with opposing fans. Nor am I talking about a player, booster, or coach who thinks winning is so important that cheating is justified. To be sure, those are extremes.

Successful sports teach the virtues Holtz conveys – discipline, persistence, and teamwork. .Those same virtues are very relevant to success in any work situation. When my kids play baseball or soccer or another sport, I mainly want them to have fun. At age eight, the final score doesn't concern me or other parents. But it does concern the kids. Even at eight, they want to win. They want to play well. They want to hit and catch the ball. They don't want to make a bad throw or a bad decision. They instinctively have a desire to excel.

Confronted by this as a parent, I have a choice. If my child wants to play well, I don't have to teach him that "winning isn't everything; it's the only thing," as can too often be the message we can hear about sports. I like to win and won twelve straight championships during high school.

I was miserable when I lost. Not because we lost per se, but because I saw how we could have played better. Without brainwashing my kids that they must win – which again, they don't – it would be crazy not to seize upon the opportunity to tap into their natural desire to do well and quote the wisdom of legendary winners along the way.

Lou Holtz teaches how to deal with life by noticing what you see on the field. Just review some of the chapter titles in his book, *Wins, Losses and Lessons,* which I've read about five times:

> It's Not What You Have,
> It's Who You Are
>
> Success Is a Choice You Make
>
> First Impressions Have Lasting
> Results
>
> A Day Without Learning Is A
> Day Without Living
>
> Setbacks Don't Define
> Your Goals, You Do
>
> Greatness Starts With Belief
> and Total Commitment
>
> Leading Is Easy When People
> Want To Be Led
>
> A Halfhearted Commitment
> Is Worse Than No Commitment
> At All
>
> Bad Things Sometimes Happen
> for a Good Reason
>
> Success is a Matter of Faith[99]

In each chapter, Holtz masterfully tells one story after another of examples from the locker room, practice field or game, and conveys how people – on the field or off – should live. He talks of the importance of discipline, persistence, teamwork, love, humor, faith and perspective. As one of his more famous phrases puts it: "First we will be *our* best and then we will be *the* best."[100]

I once frustrated a family member who wanted to bet on every golf hole. Both my relative and I played at most twice a year; betting on who had the lowest score on a hole seemed ridiculous to me given that the score might be in the teens. I just wanted to compete against myself to get better. This was incomprehensible to my playing partner. I fear that kind of competitive urge runs deep in many peoples' lives in many ways. Make no mistake, I always want to win every game I play or write the best book I can whenever I start a new project. What is gratifying to me, however, is that I have to push myself to be better than before.

The other aspect of Holtz I've always liked was his restraint. Now I've never been in a locker room with him, so I can only rely on what others have conveyed. But his practices, it seems, were tough. An exacting taskmaster, Holtz once said his objective in practice was to unify the team against a common enemy: himself.[101]

Yet during the games, you rarely saw Holtz yell at a player unless they'd been unsportsmanlike. I remember seeing him yank on a player's facemask on the sideline after the player had behaved badly. Holtz wanted his players to remain positive in the heat of the game; a mistake was much more likely to result in an arm around a kid's shoulders. I've always thought that coaches could learn a great deal from this kinder, gentler approach.

These seemingly routine, small actions add up. They also contribute to what we are known for, what we stand for and how we are perceived. That includes how teams and universities (and other businesses, governments and non-profits) act. The way they act creates their identities and provides examples to others.

When I was on the faculty at Michigan, the President of the University appointed me to a special committee that oversaw the licensees of Michigan apparel and other branded goods. At the time, Cal, Harvard, Michigan, Notre Dame and North Carolina (in no particularly order other than alphabetically) had their names on the most apparel. Licensees contractually agreed that its workers would be treated fairly according to a number of criteria. Our job was to keep tabs on those licensees and hold them accountable for their actions.

It was a tough job. Sitting in Ann Arbor, it was hard to know exactly what factories were 10,000 miles away were doing. If we received a letter complaining about a factory, we would follow up. We even worked with a few NGOs to try to be more effective. I'm sure the folks at ND were doing much the same because we all wanted to protect our brand and good name and to prevent (or at least limit) the poor treatment of people working to create goods with our names on them. Why? Because *our name means something.*

Notre Dame (and Michigan and other brands) are themselves meaningful in how business can and should be done. I try to remember that when I'm dressed in an ND shirt in a checkout line. My behavior will reflect on my alma mater in some way. Things that take place beyond the stadium matter. When I lived in places like Ann Arbor and Bloomington and even Chicago and Washington, I didn't want any poor behavior on my part to make someone think, "There's an asshole from Notre Dame."

Sports teach us lessons of life – how to analyze things, how to make sense of where we are. They're not just games that provide entertainment; they teach us what life itself is about even though we know games differ significantly from real life. These lessons have sociological dimensions such as finding identity and meaning, and even ask deep philosophical and spiritual questions.

Sports are often so central to peoples' lives that they define life itself. Take Franklin Foer's book *How Soccer Explains the World*.[102] While I never paid any attention to soccer as a kid or even as an adult, both my sons play and love the game. They even dress in international jerseys. My middle child, the oldest boy, is adopted from Ethiopia, so he has some Ethiopian soccer jerseys. My wife is 100% Czech, so my youngest, our biological child, wears a Czech jersey. (If he tried to wear his father's heritage, he'd have quite a mess given my mutt credentials.). Had our daughter played, she likely would own a jersey from her native China.

The boys love the game and eagerly follow World Cup and Olympic matches. They also have some college excellence to follow, given that Notre Dame's women's team has won three national championships and finished second five times since 1995, while the men's team won the title in 2013. What's more, my current employer, Indiana University, has won eight national championships in men's soccer, the most recent in 2012. So it's pretty easy for my sons to get excited about the sport. So I try to learn more about the game. And while I don't understand the strategies or appreciate the techniques as much as I should, I certainly witness the impact soccer has on the world.

Foer describes how soccer teams no longer rely on home-grown talent; like multinational corporations, they import it from around the globe. Ambitious business people have used ownership of sports franchises to build their political profiles and run for office. Sports can also be an outlet for the oppressed, such as when Iranian women refused to be banned from soccer matches by their regime.

Foer even uses soccer to explain culture wars, arguing that the most passionate sports fan bases are built into the working classes. While baseball, football and basketball hold the most sway in the United States, soccer is rooted in working class passion, participation, and fandom in most of the rest of the world. Ironically, when soccer in the U.S. is often championed by suburban snobs, he says, this only exacerbates class and cultural divisions. Whether he is right or wrong in that classification, he is exceptionally confident that sports can effectively explain this cultural phenomenon.

Foer's book examines a dimension of sports fandom that on a typical day is hooliganism or gangsterism, a far cry from the more benign *us vs. them*. Foer begins with the story of Red Star Belgrade, who not only meet at matches to fight other gangs, they even burst into the team's locker room to beat up players for not trying hard enough. In V-shaped formation they plough through the stadium, fighting anyone in their way. Using guerilla tactics, they dress in the opposition's jerseys and sit with opposing fans, befriend them, invite them out after the game and systematically beat them. The Red Star soccer gangs– the Bad Boys and the Ultra Bad Boys – were organized and became critical to the Serbian army during the Balkan Wars in the early 1990s.

One of the reason we are fans is that we want to be part of something and have a sense of community, if not friendship and alliances with others.[103] As Foer notes, sociologists have ascribed the rising violence at soccer games to men who have lost their jobs – or are threatened by losing them – due to the globalization of industrialization, which transports jobs to other countries, making these Bad Boys feel like emasculated, unemployed boiling pots of frustration. Soccer gangs provide identity and a release for masculine frustration. But, Foer argues, that doesn't explain the entire epidemic since some members of these groups are college kids, day-time stockbrokers and other middle class men seeking excitement.

Ugly chants, often charged with racism, religious bigotry and nationalism are part of this phenomenon. Players are expected to join in even when (as in the "Old Firm" rivalry between Glasgow, Scotland's Rangers and its Catholic Celtic team), some of the "Protestant Team's" players are actually Catholic. Foer relates that during one game, a roofer sitting next to him in the stands pointed to the field and characterized it as "good vs evil."[104]

Sometimes, "sentimental hooligans" don't have the passions of Yugoslavia or the Catholic-Protestant rivalries of Ireland and Scotland. After Margaret Thatcher declared war on soccer hooligans, electric fences in stadiums separated fans, who claimed they were being treated like animals. The battle against hooliganism, however, ultimately led to the construction of much safer soccer stadiums whose economics left no room for hooliganism. Fans of the Chelsea soccer team no longer had a stadium where they could fight, so now gangs call each other up and schedule fights instead. For these hooligans, fighting is simply a way of life.

There are many issues at play here, such as those relating to identity and the economic and cultural displacement that fuels frustrations the passions of a sports contest can stoke and release. Fighting could be a vehicle for expression of political and cultural sentiments that can't be expressed elsewhere. And it can be that some groups of men just like to pummel each other whether there is a game or not. Foer argues that "[o]f course, soccer isn't the same as Bach or Buddhism. But it is often more deeply felt than religion and just as much a part of the community's fabric, a repository of traditions."[105]

Hooliganism per se stands apart from both sport and religion and can be better described as an independent desire by some who simply lust for blood and violence. Sport and religion may even be highjacked by hooligans for their own purposes. Nothing about soccer suggests that a group of thugs brawl their way through opposing fans or befriend and lure them to another location to beat them senseless. The same can be said for religion, which has been appropriated by many a hooligan to commit atrocities in a pathetic sense of "good vs evil."

It is true, though, that sports entail traditions, identities and passions. And indeed, there are some who have made the link between theology/philosophy and sports.

Philosopher Paul Weiss argues that one important reason sports attract us is that "a superb performance interests us even more because it reveals to us the magnitude of what can be done.[106]" We don't casually admire excellence; it calls on something inside us to participate and generates our devotion. Weiss says that "we feel as though we ourselves had personally achieved something. By representing us, the athlete makes all of us be vicariously completed men."[107] He continues, "It is sport that catches the interest and elicits the devotion of both the young and the old, the wise and the foolish, the educated and the uneducated."[108]

Sports touch something deep in us and are set off as sacred. Weiss notes, "Before the game begins one salutes the flag, stands at attention, sings the national anthem, shakes hands, etc. These are the opening ceremonies serving both to hold the game away from the daily world and to direct one into the game."[109] Noting the connection between sports and war, Weis argues:

> Both war and game aim at victory. Both usually end in a clearly evidenced superiority of one side over the other, though draws and stalemates are not unknown. Only games *must* conform to rules, though in modern times we try to make wars conform to them too. But it is paradoxical to expect both sides in a war to submit to common rules. Each side seeks to annihilate the other; it would be foolish for either to allow its efforts to be restrained or blocked by an effort to conform to rules it has agreed, with its enemy, to abide by.[110]

Others have noted how baseball is indeed more than a game, and even provides a time and place to teach moral values. "It has come to symbolize national virtues of freedom, justice and equality."[111] Sports allow us to transcend ourselves and our situation and in a way, even allow our minds and perhaps our souls to levitate from our bodies. In those moments, we see that what happens in sports also occurs elsewhere. We can learn from sports and apply those lessons, virtues, and experiences to our political, business, community and religious lives.

There is a richness in this, though that richness is sometimes buried under bikini-clad advertising for potato chips and beer. To be a fan is to be a little crazy, sure, but it also grabs a bit more of us. Magic Johnson says that "to *really* watch a game you have to think like a player."[112] And that's the point. To watch is to also to play. And you don't play at just one thing. You play even when the game on television has ended because you still have lessons from the game at hand to apply to what you do next. How we watch a game has significance then, as it did for me as a nine year old who learned not to boo, but instead have a balanced approach to the game. As Bill Russell, one of the most dominant players in the NBA during the 1960s put it, "Enjoyment of a sport's artistry requires a sophistication on the part of the spectator."[113]

In short, sports teach us spiritual truths. Sports and play are so natural to us that we are inevitably drawn into games. When we are drawn into those games, we face winning and losing, what the rules are, what it means to be a good sport, how fun the moment itself can be, and what we take away from the event itself. All we have to do is to see what is right in front of us.

It's hard to think of many schools that can match Notre Dame's impact. Given Notre Dame's history, glamor and reputation, people notice it. Domers are influential, so what is said at and about Notre Dame easily transfers to our jobs, our families and the other games we play. That's why we ask athletes to be role models. Otherwise, it doesn't make much sense for people to be role models just because they can kick or throw a ball. But we fans (and players) end up investing so much energy and passion into sports and play we yearn to translate - in words and action - what we see on the field to other areas of life. We feel deeply disappointed when that passion turns negative or scandalous.

I believe we often make too much of scandal, not because scandal is unimportant, but rather because the real lesson is how we practice the virtues we admire. We can admire the positive actions of players, coaches and teams. When we take those virtues to heart, the virtues themselves become the thing we can treasure rather than the perfection (or lack thereof) of a given player, coach or team. I don't mind sports heroes; I've had many. But when I was locked in the stadium, I wasn't thinking about the greatness of any particular player, coach or even Notre Dame football itself. I was thinking about what being in that Stadium and being part of that university taught me. Those lessons went well beyond football.

CHAPTER SIX

To Every Thing There is a Season

Notre Dame's first intercollegiate athletic contest took place against Michigan in 1887. In the 128 years since, Notre Dame has won eleven NCAA-recognized consensus national championships in football, with eight other squads achieving national championships as well. (This does not count some recognition given to the 1993 team, who definitely should have been acknowledged as national champions, or the odd top-ranking to the 2012 team by the Colley Matrix computer poll even after Alabama clobbered us.) [114] Notre Dame has also won championships in sixteen other sports seasons, led by fencing with seven and soccer, four. Three other titles can be claimed but they were before NCAA recognition standards were established, including basketball in 1927 and 1936.[115] If you count all of these, they would amount to 38 championships in 128 years or, on average, one every 3.37 years. That's frequent enough so that on average, during a four-year college residency, an ND student could claim the Irish were #1.

You can narrow this further. Notre Dame's first national championship came in 1924. So, in the last 91 years (as of this writing), ND's 38 national championships amount to a title every 2.39 years.

Notre Dame's history gives ample reason to claim #1 status in football, which is the winningest program (by percentage) in college football history. Knute Rockne is the all-time winningest coach (again by percentage) in college football history, followed by Frank Leahy. Notre Dame has the most members of the College Football Hall of Fame and the most consensus first team All-Americans.

As of this writing, Notre Dame has had the best graduation rate (99%) for all sports for eight consecutive years.[116] Notre Dame and Georgetown alternate as the No. 1 Catholic institution for higher learning in the *Times Higher Education* World University Rankings.[117] Bloomberg *Businessweek* consistently ranks The Mendoza College of Business at Notre Dame in the top five and occasionally #1 for its undergraduate program.[118] Of course, there are many other markers that place Notre Dame in the top 5, 10 or 20 in other academic, alumni, sports and other rankings, so there is certainly much to be proud of and plenty of bragging rights Domers can claim.

Yet some worry that Notre Dame's glory (in football anyway) has come and gone. A fellow Domer who was on Michigan's faculty with me was concerned that we had become like Michigan, which spent nearly 50 years between national championships. They, too, had a storied history, and were an iconic, Midwest-based program, but not one that was going to contend with the SEC or warm-weather universities where elite athletes want to play. While I reject that notion, the truth is that as of this writing, it has been 29 years since our 1988 title. We're more than halfway to that once-in-a-half-century mark.

ND's excellence and achievements, however, are not why I kiss the grass when I return to campus. Nor is it, I strongly suspect, the reason for the loyalty of other ND alums. Beyond the rankings, we kiss the grass because we learned so much about the importance of discipline and the need to follow rules. We also developed a sense for when rules should be challenged, but that – when done well – requires even more discipline.

What's more, we learned how to treat others as we would like to be treated, not in a formulaic way, but in a truly genuine manner. Were there rivalries and fights? Sure. But there was also a sense that we all shared in something special, one reason alumni satisfaction at ND is in the top three in the country.[119] We experienced just how special ND is. When you stepped back from the pressures of exams and the day-to-day hustle and bustle, you could see that it really was as good as it gets.

We go to college to grow up, be on our own, get an education, find a significant other, bond with the Divine, and engage in life. There is a time and place for all of this, just as King Solomon said.

> To every thing there is a season, and a time to every purpose under the heaven:
> A time to be born, and a time to die; a time to plant, and a time to pluck up that which is planted;
> A time to kill, and a time to heal; a time to break down, and a time to build up;
> A time to weep, and a time to laugh; a time to mourn, and a time to dance;
> A time to cast away stones, and a time to gather stones together;
> A time to embrace, and a time to refrain from embracing;
> A time to get, and a time to lose; a time to keep, and a time to cast away;
> A time to rend, and a time to sew; a time to keep silence, and a time to speak;
> A time to love, and a time to hate; a time of war, and a time of peace.[120]

Many times, going to a game is an escape, a chance to let off some steam from the pressures of the world. There will be a time to cheer your heart out and pull so hard for your team that it seems there is nothing more important in the world. There is also the recognition that all of these lessons in life can be demonstrated by the teams we watch play.

Times and seasons suggest a certain rhythm. After all, the seasons come and go on a regular, predictable basis and result from laws of nature. Domers can rely on these kinds of cycles and get carried away by them. The best example I can think of is the notion that great coaches win the national championship in their third year.

If you look at ND history, Rockne, Leahy, Parseghian, Devine and Holtz all won championships in their third year at the helm. Brian Kelly took the Irish to a national championship game in his third year. Coaches at other schools have done something similar and Ara himself said that by the third year, you can usually figure out the trajectory of a program. We Domers, then, tend to be pretty focused on what our coaches do in their third year.

In many ways, this notion makes sense. A new coach always has to establish himself. At times, a coach may need to turn a team around. In 2010, the chatter floating around the stands was that the Irish had forgotten how to win and needed to pay attention to little things that end up making big differences. So it was not surprising to see Brian Kelly erupt on the sidelines each week as he willed the players into paying attention and being focused. Time and again, the cameras panned to Kelly vociferously addressing a shortcoming.

You could argue that Kelly took things too far, but in that telling third year, we sat 12-0, ranked #1 and heading into the national championship game. Apparently, there was a time and season for Kelly's tactics. That 2012 team seemed about as mentally tough as any Irish team I ever followed.

Other times, the laws of nature don't apply so well. After all, Ara was a blown call or two from winning a national championship in his *first* year, two years ahead of schedule. Sometimes, there aren't any good reasons for the rules we think will to lead to victory, including those serial underpants changers. That may explain why, at this writing, many people are excited about the Triple Crown Winner in horse racing: apparently, Notre Dame has done well when a horse wins the Triple Crown.[121]

We live by these kinds of informal methods and ideas. That's OK. Nature is full of predictability. The regularity of seasons, stages of life, behaviors that sustain relationships and disciplines that make us better all carry over into sports. But life's a little too complex to be fully compartmentalized in this way.

One of the harder principles of nature to get right is balance. Life is full of tugs and pulls – balancing family and work, loyalty and honesty – and knowing what to do at a given time requires real wisdom, what Aristotle called *phronesis*. Things that have become unbalanced in sports require some re-balancing as well.

Many complain that college and pro sports are out of hand and that players aren't setting good examples. Some of our heroes are not that heroic after all. Performance-enhancing drugs, academic cheating, off-field criminal behavior and even betting undermine the integrity of the game. It's tough to explain to children (or grown-ups for that matter) why we should look up to some sports figures.

When we see scandals and failures, however, we are simply seeing ourselves. Players and coaches are humans too. Fans are as much a part of the corrosiveness of money in sports as any agent or shady booster. *We* watch the games on ESPN and NBC, buy the tickets and wear the sweatshirts that encourage us to "Play Like a Champion." When we see players, coaches and teams that fail, it's better to consider how those failures reflect us than it is to tut-tut about the players. When we see players and schools that get things right, we should celebrate and recognize that if these players and institutions can do things right, so can we.

As fans, while we may learn from sports, our lives can impact sports as well. It's not enough to whine about scandals; fans have a role in changing behavior. All sports teams have to account for issues such as player safety (particularly concussions) and off-field violence. Technology has helped us with issues that otherwise might have been missed. Brain scanning technology highlights the damage of concussions and security cameras make incidents of domestic violence much more transparent. Leagues and teams value their reputation and brand, so public pressure can help the game and the athletes.

Players seem to realize this. On occasion, pitchers intentionally hit batters to defend a teammate who has been hit by the opposing pitcher or taken out too hard on a slide. After a recent death in the cricket world, one commentator said retaliations of this kind – in cricket and baseball – should simply be outlawed. In an interview, pitcher David Price said he thought defending a teammate was important but that there is a difference between hitting an opposing player low and throwing a 95 mile an hour fastball at his head.

I tried to learn from prominent professional pitchers of my day when I was growing up, but I don't recall anyone making that kind of distinction between types of payback pitches. I used to throw high and inside before it dawned on my obviously poorly-developing brain that I was flirting with another person's death. But whether it is public pressure or a moral sentiment learned elsewhere in life, the outside world impacts sports. What we do and learn and how we behave as fans and citizens makes a difference in games.

The criticism made against the deterioration in sports and its ethics, however, stems from the observation that there is too much money involved in sports. [122] But marketing is the primary reason behind the money in sports, which means that fans can contribute to the integrity of the game. If fans want to claim credit for causing an offside penalty because the opposing team's linemen can't hear his quarterback's cadence, then why can't they take more responsibility for the integrity of the game itself?

You may think that individual fans don't have very much power but I happened to be driving from Ann Arbor to South Bend the day Ty Willingham, head coach of the Irish from 2002-2004, was fired. Willingham, of course, had a very disappointing tenure but I strongly felt – and still believe – that he should have been given a full five years like other Irish coaches in the last fifty years. So I went over to the office of Monk Malloy, then President of Notre Dame.

I lived upstairs from Malloy at Sorin Hall my senior year and occasionally received phone calls and visits from him about on my habit of dribbling the basketball on the floor. While I doubted if he remembered me, I believed we had enough of a connection that he might see me and hear my protest. He was out of the office, so I wrote a four-page letter complaining about Willingham's firing. I also refused to go to a game for the rest of Willingham's original contract. Did this have an impact? Well, it did for me. Any action we take has to start with us.

I did not enjoy teaching Executive MBA students, even though my courses were well-received. At times I've felt that EMBA students had too high of an opinion of themselves and their experience and demanded to be served rather than taught. I had no patience for that. I figured a bunch of pro football players would amp these problems into the stratosphere.

I couldn't have been more wrong. The students/players were fantastic. Hard working. Intelligent. Supportive of each other. Highly disciplined. Granted, a group of guys who have been out of college for ten years playing in the NFL who took the time to work for an advanced degree would logically be the cream of the crop. That cream was still impressive. I was ashamed of my hesitation to teach them. Simply ashamed, and I told them so.

The interesting thing about reputation, as I tell my ethics students, is that it is an asset recorded on the books of a business that is held by someone else. Most players are, in fact, concerned about their reputations and wince when others bring the NFL brand down through bad behavior.

Notre Dame is hardly perfect.[123] Some of the recent academic misfires concern me and, though I have read the news stories, I do not understand how a twenty year old gets onto a fifty foot tower in fifty mile per hour winds to film a practice. And then dies. Others will have additional questions about things that happen, as well they should. None of us is perfect and there will be times when things go wrong and even more when questions arise. Overall, though, I think Notre Dame really tries to get things right and, on the whole, does a pretty good job. That's worth championing as well.

All of this makes Notre Dame #1. Does it mean that we are better than everyone else? Sometimes and in some things, yes. When we beat West Virginia in the 1989 Fiesta Bowl, we were indeed better than everyone else. In over 128 years, we have the best record in college football, the most members of the Hall of Fame, the most consensus All-Americans and arguably the most national championships, so yes, in those ways we are better than everyone else.

When we graduate athletes for eight straight years at a better rate than anyone else does, we deserve to claim we are better at that too, which adds further luster to our athletic successes. Some of the coaches whose win-loss records at Notre Dame disappointed have contributed to this success. I have never heard complaints on this score about Gerry Faust, Bob Davie, Willingham or Weis. Giving credit for those contributions is a #1 approach.

When we recognize that another school has done better than we have and we congratulate them, we may be #1 in sportsmanship too. When we print tee-shirts that celebrate the game rather than using an expletive for the other team (the unfortunate *Catholics vs. Convicts* the exception), we're better than those who denigrate opposing teams. When our coaches take lessons from sports life and translate them into terms that help people live better and fruitful lives, we are in league with other notables – Coach K at Duke comes to mind – who do this exceptionally well.

Notre Dame is #1 in my book and this book. Notre Dame is #1 in a lot of places. Without turning a blind eye toward things that need to be improved, I'd like to see supporters from all teams dig into their school's history to demonstrate how they have done well in wins-losses, discipline, sportsmanship, absorbing the full atmosphere of the moment, and seeing how the positive lessons they discover apply to other aspects of life. That would be awesome and uplifting in many different ways.

There's one thing left to cover though. Did God *really* make Notre Dame #1? If God chooses to make Notre Dame #1, then does that mean God doesn't love other schools? Why insert the Divine into this picture at all?

When I was that nine year old kid booing the other team, I saw God as my grandfather saw Ara Parseghian: As an old, wise, gentle figure.

When I played sports, I learned about the rules that lead to success, like running wind springs until I threw up or passed out without a coach yelling at me. I knew that a 5'8" 150 pound kid stood no chance unless I was really disciplined in my training. One of my favorite Biblical stories is the lesson of the talents, which says that those who get the most out of their talents receive the most rewards.

Through all of this, a good family, community and university taught me the importance of the Golden Rule. Treating others as I hoped to be treated aligned well with sportsmanship (not to mention golden helmets and Domes). So my vision of the Divine increasingly included the karma of justice.

As I received my advanced education, I was continually amazed at just how rich the world is; life, the universe, beauty. I had to stop and realize I was never going to understand it all, but with gratitude, I could recognize all the wonders of life and nature that surrounded me. It was then that I started to also think of the Divine as a Star Wars (or Buddhist-like) force that permeated our entire existence. I saw how so many different theological paths might lead to the Divine. So could non-theistic paths.

When I became a father relatively late in life, I continued to notice many lessons that applied elsewhere in life. My two-year old's anger at my discipline was replicated by my equally (im)mature anger at God when I didn't get *my* way. With children adopted from Asia and Africa, I began to recognize similar notions in other cultures, nations and traditions. The Divine popped up in so many unexpected ways I couldn't keep count. The goodness of these connections blends both our reason and our emotions. They appeal to our good nature deep inside us and resonate in our bones. Sadly, the wisdom of our emotions is a bit lost today.

Sports help us get back to these emotions and teach us some spiritual truths. We can't just rely on emotions of course; if we did, we'd have to say that the emotions that prompted that Oklahoma fan to squeeze the testicles out of the Longhorn fan might be OK.[124] But I do think that a balance between reason and emotions helps us in the world today. I also believe that Notre Dame, exactly because of this mix of emotions, reason and sports has much to teach us and it's this aspect of Notre Dame's greatness that connects us with the Divine.

It certainly doesn't get better than that.

CHAPTER SEVEN

How God Made Notre Dame #1

No, I am not going to try to prove whether or not God exists.[125]

Instead, I'd ask you to remember the old 1980s film, *Angels in the Outfield*. A charming movie with a totally predictable script, a kid looks to have a family when his father cannot take care of him. He stumbles into the irascible manager of the California Angels, played by Danny Glover, who heads a pathetic team. The kid starts to see angels who miraculously transform the baseball Angels into championship material. The impact of the boy also draws Glover's attention, and he begins to get close to the little boy and his also-orphaned friend. The kids let everyone know that angels are actually helping the Angels; in the championship game, everyone hopes for heavenly help.

The washed-up pitcher, played by Tony Danza, is worn out in the ninth, but just one pitch away from the win. Glover refuses Danza's plea to come out, telling him that an angel is ready to help him with the last pitch. Emboldened by this and thousands of fans, waving their arms in the "I see an angel" signal, Danza reaches back and retires the final batter. After the game, Glover tells Danza there was no angel and that Danza delivered himself. Because of his *belief* that he had help, he prevailed.

It's an old Hollywood theme; Even Dumbo the elephant believed the impossible – that he, an elephant, could fly – because of a magic feather. When the feather flew away, Dumbo fell towards the earth until his mouse-companion convinced him the feather was just a trick to give him confidence. Dumbo could fly the whole time. Convinced, he soared again.

Does the Divine really intercede in the outfield? Wouldn't the Almighty have better things to do than play ball? Perhaps, but maybe an ordinary event is the way to get into people's hearts and minds. God relentlessly loves us and will never stop reaching out to us, a key reason I am so open to different religious traditions. I believe the Lord never gives up on us; it's just up to us to accept help. If that is true of religions around the world, why couldn't it be true in sports? Or music…or welding…or anything else where the Divine can reach us?

Belief in something more powerful than yourself is a pretty powerful thing. Scores of psychologists and even more self-help gurus help people eliminate crippling fears that prevent them from doing what they might do if they weren't so afraid. A belief that the Almighty is on your shoulder when shooting a hockey puck or when your team is making a last-minute comeback melts a lot of fear

This is one way to see that God really did make Notre Dame #1. If you *believe* that God is on your side, then maybe s/he really does stretch out that arm to catch the fly ball in the outfield. Or maybe just believing that the most powerful force in the universe is on your side makes you willing to leap a little farther. The freedom in your kick as you try for that 50 yard field goal might be a little greater. The three-pointer you launch might be a bit surer. The class you teach or the client you represent or the patient you treat might come into a sharper focus.

A place like my alma mater is ready-made for this kind of belief because religious devotion is so central to the identity of the campus. It's an easy reach to think that God made Notre Dame #1 when the team walks directly from Sacred Heart Basilica to the locker room to put on the pads. But even without that institutional support for belief in God, we humans fall very easily into those *us vs. them* patterns that prompt us to call on extra help when we need to, even if it is at the expense of the other guy. If God is God of all, then that force is available to more than just those whose campuses have a basilica within sight of the stadium. God may very well have made a lot of people #1; they simply need to open up and let the angels play ball with them.

There have been centuries of debate as to whether this belief is an illusion or real. I decidedly choose to believe the latter. If you choose the former, though, there remains some kind of force or confidence accessible through belief that is still pretty powerful. Whether or not you associate that power with the Divine doesn't necessarily remove that force. This is one reason I believe other universities that do not have an explicit religious foundation might still be able to find spiritual lessons by studying sports. Explicit faith in the Divine makes these connections easier to see and more profound, but I think that relentless spiritual essence is there no matter what.

The Jewish Kabbalah asserts that belief in the Divine creates a pathway for the believer but also for others who follow the belief. Once any given person believes in a transcendent being, a road already exists. People also connect with the Divine through actions, so each time a person takes an action of love, generosity, peace, respect or many others, not only does that person connect with the Divine, but their efforts also make it easier for others to follow a now-established path. This puts to the side the *faith vs works* debate Christians have engaged in over millennia, and helps us see that spiritual truths connect us to a transcendent Force. Sports, in their part, demonstrate those truths.

As we've seen, there are other spiritual connections available during sporting events. That's because sports are, as one scholar put it, natural religions:

> Sports flow outward into action from a deep natural impulse that is radically religious: an impulse of freedom, respect for ritual limits, a zest for symbolic meaning, and a longing for perfection. The athlete may of course be pagan, but sports are, as it were, natural religions. There are many ways to express this radical impulse: by the asceticism and decision of preparation; by a sense of respect for the mysteries of one's own body and soul, and for powers not in one's own control; by a sense of awe for the place and time of competition; by a sense of fate; by a felt sense of comrade-ship and destiny; by a sense of participation in the rhythms and tides of nature itself."[126]

Michael Novak may have analyzed the religious aspects of sports more than anyone else has. He writes that legendary announcer Howard Cosell challenged him to prove that football is more than mere entertainment.[127] Novak argued that sports were more serious than entertainment, which he said is what happens at halftime or on a television at a hotel bar. Sports, though, "make the men around the same bar silent, reverent, elated or despondent on Monday nights as the last quarter brings on the game's climatic moments."[128]

Others have suggested that sports convey spiritual dimensions that religion often doesn't. Quoting former New York Governor Mario Cuomo, two scholars argue that while the Bible might encourage us to find individual fulfillment in the success of our community, a winning team does a far better job.[129]

What's more, sports tap into a dimension of our nature that we share with other animals. To play is to have a sense of joy; that can range well beyond rules and winning. If the insight from the Kabbalah is correct, then engaging in this play allows us to pave that pathway to the Divine, making interaction with the Divine easier for us and for others who follow.

Let me review what I've tried to lay out regarding the spiritual truths we find in sports. First, there is the importance of joining with others, even when that involves being "against" someone else – the *us vs. them* perspective I've pointed out many times. Then, there is the importance of rules and discipline as well as sportsmanship. The awareness of the specialness of what is transpiring is another truth that arises in sports, as does the way in which actions on the field translate to everyday life. Finally, there is the freedom to move among these truths to enjoy and learn different things at different times and seasons.

These spiritual truths reveal how God made Notre Dame #1. God really does cheer for old Notre Dame. God is on Notre Dame's side of the ball and on Notre Dame's sideline all the time. It's just that God might be on Michigan's sideline as well. ND might feel freer to claim God's support because its religious tradition teaches that God generally does support us so when good things happen to us, it's not outlandish to recognize what has been taught to believers for a long time. Religions always have to deal with the fact that sometimes things don't go so well. When that's the case, a little mettle testing may need to occur. God, though, is still with us.

Some relatives once talked about the need for a college football playoff. I could care less about the idea. If it happens, fine, but I'm also fine without it. In fact, I'd prefer the old days to the screwed up BCS system. But they believed there HAD to be just one #1 team at the end of the season.

"Why?" I asked.

They were dumbfounded by my question. The discussion occurred not too long after Michigan and Nebraska both laid claim to the 1997 National Championship. It seemed to me fine that they both claimed to be #1. Exactly who was harmed by a controversy? For that matter, with all due respect to March Madness or any other playoff system, do we really think that the best team wins or is it just that the right team gets hot during a certain month of the year? I am OK with a few national champions. Similarly, I can believe that God completely loves Michigan and Texas and Northwestern.

Miami? That's a different story.

Seriously, God even loves Miami.

The trouble isn't that God made Notre Dame #1; the trouble is that in our *us vs. them* spirituality, it's hard to recognize how God also made Texas and Northwestern and Miami #1. Our *us vs. them* eyes see God's support for us, but we don't see that support for others. Though this may seem innocuous enough, millions of human beings have been slaughtered because each side only saw God's support for them and their cause without recognizing that God's support for them didn't mean God didn't love their enemy as well.

One of the things that separates Notre Dame from other places is that its religious identity makes Domers more open to the idea that God is interested in human beings and that a Divine Force surges through us. In that sense, *God Made Notre Dame #1* is not a boast; it's a humble moment of gratitude as well as a recognition that we are connected to an amazing Force that is there to help us. That's pretty cool stuff.

My unquestioned belief is that Force is available to everyone. My challenge is that other schools, universities and others try to articulate just how God made *them* #1. Doing so takes nothing away from Notre Dame; in fact, my love of Notre Dame has lead me to help others recognize something amazing in and beyond themselves.

In short, God really did make Notre Dame #1. And God did it by making everyone else #1 too.

INDEX

1812 Overture, 10, 75
A Few Good Men, 53
Alabama, 28, 49, 66, 120
Allen, Ray, 81
America the Beautiful, 85
Angels in the Outfield, 131
Annapolis, 50
Annapolis West, 50
Apollo 9, 101
Argentina, 7
Aristotle, 94, 124
Arjuna, 19
Army, 47, 48, 52, 53, 54
As Good As It Gets, 18, 20, 31, 32, 38, 41, 42, 83, 89, 122
Atlantic Coast Conference(ACC), 56, 75
Ave Maria, 67
Band of the Fighting Irish, 84
Banuelos, Francisco, 61
Basking in Reflected Glory, 80
Beaver Stadium, 94
Belden, Tony, 45
Benedict, 9
Benton High School, 60
Bhagavad, Gita, 19
Big Ten, 50, 82
Bispo, Randall, 61
Blimp, 18, 20, 24, 99, 103
Boston Celtics, 80, 81
Boston College, 30
Bowden, Bobby, 79
Brady, Tom, 22, 37
Brickhouse, Jack, 87

Bridgewater State, 59
Brindza, Kyle, 70
Brownback, Sam, 107
Bryant, Bear, 28, 66
Buddhism, 37, 116
Burke, Peter J., 149
Bush, George H.W., 101
Bush, George W, 100
Businessweek, 121
BYU, 79, 80
Camus, Albert, 86
Carey, Harry, 87
Carmel High School, 61, 62
Carr, Lloyd, 34, 35
Carroll, Pete, 68, 90
Carthage College, 69
Catholicism, 13
Catholics vs Convicts, 64, 73, 128
Chelsea, 115
Chicago Bulls, 75, 88
Chicago Cubs, 46, 86, 87, 88
Chicago Tribune, 88
Chicago White Sox, 76, 87, 88
Chile, 7
Christianity, 37
Cichy, Steve, 45
Cleveland Browns, 84
Clinton, Bill, 100
College Conference of Illinois and Wisconsin
   Swimming Championship, 69
College Football Hall of Fame, 27, 120
Colley Matrix, 120
Connecticut (University of), 92, 93
Corzatt, Mike, 21, 22
Cosell, Howard, 49, 134
Cotton Bowl, 11, 44, 45, 66, 71, 82
Crowley, Jim, 48

Danza, Tony, 131
Davie, Bob, 128
Davis, Anthony, 62
Denver Broncos, 83
DePaul University, 75, 76
Detroit, 57
Detroit Tigers, 57, 86
Devine, Dan, 26, 27, 64, 66, 68, 74, 123
discipline, 9, 20, 30, 36, 38, 64, 89, 91, 99, 109, 111, 121, 129, 130, 135
Divine, 17, 27, 29, 37, 43, 46, 48, 68, 74, 122, 129, 130, 132, 133, 135, 137
Dolan, Thomas, 149
Domers, 4, 13, 15, 17, 20, 24, 56, 68, 73, 79, 97, 107, 118, 121, 123, 137
Donald, Jason, 57
Dow, Bill, 53
Dumbo, 131
Durkheim, Emile, 20
Edsall, Randy, 93
Eisenhower, Dwight, 52
England, 7
Engzell, Louise, 58
ESPN, 88, 125
Evanston, 41
Fan, 4, 5, 6, 7, 8, 9, 10, 12, 16, 17, 22, 27, 28, 32, 33, 34, 35, 36, 38, 41, 50, 52, 55, 56, 64, 66, 71, 72, 77, 78, 79, 80, 81, 82, 86, 87, 88, 89, 90, 91, 92, 94, 97, 114, 117, 130, 149
Fanatic, 92
Fanaticus, 92
Faust, Gerry, 66, 72, 128
Fiesta Bowl, 128
Fighting Irish, 37, 106

Florida State, 50, 62, 70, 74, 79
Foer, Franklin, 113, 114, 116
Forystek, Gary, 64
French Quarter, 82
Gallaraga, Arman, 57, 59
Garnett, Kevin, 81
Gator Bowl, 64
George Washington University, 96
Georgia Bulldogs, 82
Georgia, University of, 82
GeorgiaTech, 82
Gerlach, Michael, 61
Germany, 7
Gipp, George (Gipper), 101
Glee Club, 76, 95
Glover, Danny, 131
Golden Rule, 129
Gonzales, 61
Green Jersey Game, 64, 66
Griese, Bob, 34
Griffin, Archie, 54
Grotto, 97
Haines, Kris, 46
Haiti, 90
Hamilton, Remy, 30, 36, 37
Harvard, 112
Heisman Trophy, 54, 63, 79
Hesburgh Memorial Library, 51
Hesburgh, Theodore, 97
Hindu (ism), 19, 37
Holtz, Lou, 36, 41, 62, 63, 68, 72, 73, 74, 103, 107, 108, 110, 111, 123
Hooliganism, 114, 115, 116
Houston, 44, 45
Howard, Jasper, 92, 93
Hurricanes (Miami), 72, 73, 74
Ignatius of Loyola, 9

Indiana University, 42, 44, 113
Johnson, Jimmy, 72, 74
Johnson, Magic, 117
Jones, Howard, 63
Jordan, Michael, 88
Joyce ACC, 56
Joyce, Jim, 57
Judaism, 37
Kabbalah, 133, 135
Katz, Bob, 108
Kelly, Brian, 123
Kennedy, Joseph P., 102
Kiffin, Lane, 90
Knox County, 90
Koran, 9
Kosovo, 100
Kryk, John, 26
Kuharich, Joe, 68
Laden, Elmer, 48
LaVell Edwards Stadium, 80
Leahy, Frank, 68, 102, 120, 123
Levy, Linda, 149
Lincoln (Nebraska), 63
Lisch, Rusty, 64
Little Brown Jug, 85
Logan Center, 62
Longhorn, 7, 11, 71, 72, 130
Los Angeles, 33, 82
Los Angeles Lakers, 80, 88
Lynch, Dick, 49
Madrid, Manuel, 61
Manning, Peyton, 90
Marquette University, 75
Mary, 14, 26, 31
Maryville, 60, 61
McCain, John, 100
McCamy, Dan, 60

McCarthy, Tim, 98
McKay, John, 68
MELNICK, 149
Mets (New York), 107
Michigan, 11, 23, 25, 26, 27, 29, 30,
    31, 32, 33, 34, 35, 36, 37, 38, 39,
    40, 41, 42, 50, 55, 62, 72, 73, 81,
    85, 106, 112, 120, 121, 135, 136
Midshipmen, 52, 53
Miller, 48
Milwaukee Brewers, 76
Monk, Edward (Monk), 126
Montana, Joe, 21, 22, 27, 37, 45, 46, 47,
    64, 66, 103
National Anthem, 76, 83, 85, 117
Navy, 50, 51, 52, 53, 54, 62, 88
NBC, 15, 75, 125
NCAA, 42, 69, 84, 120
New Year's Eve, 49, 82
New York Yankees, 56
NFL, 47, 52, 66, 78, 84, 88, 127
Nicholson, Jack, 53
Nitz, Jonothan, 69
North Carolina (University of), 77, 112
Northwestern University, 27, 41, 42, 106
Notre Dame Victory March, 39
Novak, Michael, 134
Obama, Barack, 99
Ohio State, 11, 48, 54, 55, 62
Oklahoma, 7, 48, 107, 130
Ole Miss, 64, 90
Oliver, Harry, 26, 29, 30, 32, 36, 37, 81
Orange Bowl, 49, 82
Pac 8, 82
Palafox, Alberto, 61
Palin, Sarah, 100
Parseghian, Ara, 11, 12, 44, 49, 68, 101,

102, 123, 129
Paxson, John, 89
Pekin, 5
Penn State, 50, 64, 72, 94
Peru, 7
Phelps, Digger, 28, 62, 65, 66, 67, 74, 76
Phillies (Philadelphia), 107
Pierce, Paul, 81
Pietrosante, Nick, 49
Pilney, Joe, 48
Pittsburgh Steelers, 66
Pittsburgh, University of (Pitt), 50, 64
Play Like a Champion, 36, 107, 125
Pope, 14
Presbyterian, 12
Price, David, 125
Purdue, 49, 50, 62, 64, 72
Putnam, 15
Reagan, Ronald, 101
Red Sox, 56, 87
Red Star Belgrade, 114
religion, 9, 14, 16, 20, 37, 49, 116, 134
Reynolds, Tucker, 59
Rice Eccles Stadium, 80
Rice, Grantland, 48
Rice, Tony, 64
Robinson, John, 65, 67, 68
Rockne, Bonnie, 63
Rockne, Knute, 101, 102, 120
Romney, Mitt, 99
Rose Bowl, 35, 41, 82
Rothenbaum, Isaac, 69
Rudolph, Will, 61
Rue, Loyal, 9
rules, 17, 18, 20, 24, 29, 31, 36, 39, 42, 53, 54, 55, 56, 57, 59, 64, 77,

83, 89, 91, 101, 117, 118, 121, 124, 135
Russell, Bill, 118
Sampson, Ralph, 75
San Francisco (University of), 75, 76
Schembechler, Bo, 36
Schmitz, Mike, 21, 22
Seminoles, Florida State, 79
Shakespeare, Bill, 48
Sisyphus, 86, 87
Snow Bowl, 50
Solomon, King, 19, 122
Sooner, 7
Sorin Hall, 47, 126
Sousa, John Philip, 39
South Africa, 7, 95
South Bend, 11, 36, 48, 67, 68, 79, 94, 95, 126
South Bend Tribune, 98
Southeast Conference, 82
Southwest conference, 82
Spirituality, 9, 14, 16, 17, 18, 19, 20, 23, 29, 32, 40, 43, 83, 136
Sports Illustrated, 44
Sportsmanship, 18, 20, 24, 51, 53, 54, 55, 56, 57, 59, 69, 70, 78, 89, 93, 128, 129, 135
St. Joseph, Missouri, 60
Stepan Center, 65
Stets, Jan E., 149
Stickles, Monty, 48
Stronghurst Zippers, 5, 6
Stuhldreher, 48
Sugar Bowl, 28, 49, 53, 81
Sullivan, Joe, 48
Take Me out to the Ballgame, 85
Taoism, 37

Tennessee (University of), 90
Texas, 50, 62, 71, 101, 136
Thatcher, Margaret, 115
Times Higher Education, 121
Touchdown Jesus, 51
Trojan horse, 65, 74
Trojans, 22, 62, 67
Tucholsky, Sara, 77
U.S. Open, 57, 58
UCLA, 28, 75, 76
Ultra Bad Boys, 114
umpire, 56, 57, 58, 101
Unis, Joe, 46
USC (University of Southern California), 49, 62, 65, 66, 67, 68, 73, 74, 90
Utah (University of), 80
Victors, the, 39
Victory March, 13, 39, 75
Vietnam, 53
Virginia (University of), 75
Virginia Tech, 93, 94
Walker, Herschel, 82
WANN, DANIEL, 149
Wann, Daniel, 90
Ward, Charley, 79
washington, university of, 96
Waxman, Butch, 62
WBBM, 88
We are ND, 65
We Are the green Machine, 65
Weber, Robin, 49
Websters Sports Dictionary, 92
Weis, Charlie, 50, 51, 128
Weiss, Paul, 116
West Pointers, 53
West Virginia (University of), 92, 93, 128
WGN, 88

what would you fight for?, 106
Wheaton College, 69
Williams, Bobby, 49
Williams, Ollie, 95
Williams, Serena, 57, 58
Willingham, Tyrone, 126, 128
Wilson, Gyyne, 63
Wilson, Red, 107
WMAQ, 88
Wolverines, 30, 31, 32, 34, 55
Wooden, John, 28, 44
World Series, 84, 86, 87
World War II, 50, 51
Wrigley Field, 87
Ziesel, Matt, 60

ENDNOTES

[1] DANIEL L. WANN, MERRILL J. MELNICK, GORDON W. RUSSELL, & DALE G. PEASE, SPORTS FANS: THE PSYCHOLOGY AND SOCIAL IMPACT OF SPECTATORS 102 (2001).
[2] *Id.* at 102.
[3] *Id.* at 102.
[4] *Id* at 102.
[5] *Id.* at 102.
[6] *Id.* at 102.
[7] Associated Press, (September 12, 2007), accessed at http://www.foxnews.com/story/2007/09/12/texas-football-fan-nearly-castrated-in-bar-fight-in-oklahoma-bar.html
[8] *Id.*
[9] WANN et. al., *supra* note 1.
[10] Linda Levy, *A Study of Sports Crowd Behavior: The Case of the Great Pumpkin Incident* 13 JOURNAL OF SPORT & SOCIAL ISSUES 89

(1989).
[11] WANN et. al, *supra* note 1, at 98.
[12] WANN et. al., *supra* note 1, at 100.
[13] *See, e.g.* Daniel Wann, *Aggression Among Highly Identified Spectators as a Function of Their Need to Maintain Positive Social Identity* 17 JOURNAL OF SPORT AND SOCIAL ISSUES 134 (1993); Daniel Wann & Thomas Dolan, *Attributions of highly identified sports spectators* 134 THE JOURNAL OF SPORTS PSYCHOLOGY 783 (1994); and Daniel Wann, *Preliminary Validation of the Sport Fan Motivation Scale* 19 JOURNAL OF SPORT AND SOCIAL ISSUES 377 (1995).
[14] DAVID SLOAN WILSON, DARWINS'S CATHEDRAL: EVOLUTION, RELIGION, AND THE NATURE OF SOCIETY (2010).
[15] Jan E. Stets & Peter J. Burke, *Identity Theory and Social Identity Theory* 63 SOCIAL PSYCHOLOGY QUARTERLY 224 (2000).
[16] Fortunately, though our Presbyterian heritage was tied to the teachings of John Calvin, Grandpa Gibb's protestant orientation – at least with respect to sports – more followed Martin Luther. Luther was "a robust proponent of sports" whereas Calvin took a more dour view. *See,* ANDREW COOPER, PLAYING IN THE ZONE 99 (1998).
[17] See, e,g, GARRY J. SMITH, THE NOBLE SPORTS FAN 57 (1998).
[18] The ancient chakras use colors to represent spiritual progress and that color-coded model has been extended more recently by others. In this book, I am going to focus on the categories of moral and spiritual development, but if you would like to see their integration with the color-coded models, along with an application I use for a student reflection paper integrating both sports and music, you are welcome to check out the following short reading: https://iu.box.com/s/p7d41irpw8w7f92ox3tmbamw2j7277d5.
[19] DIGGER PHELPS WITH TIM BOURRET, TALES FROM THE NOTRE DAME FIGHTING IRISH LOCKER ROOM 45 (2015) at 45.
[20] *Id.* at 45.
[21] *Id.* at 46.
[22] Of course, the famous Touchdown Jesus, also known as the Word of Life mural, that rises to the north of the stadium. Even with new construction at the stadium, one can still see Touchdown Jesus from the stands.
[23] During my years at Notre Dame, the "We're #1 Moses" statue in front of the Hesburgh Memorial Library also was known as the "There Goes Hesburgh" statue. That recognized that Father Hesburgh, then in his 35 years as President of the University was deeply involved in world affairs and always, it seemed, was jetting off to other places in the world. Either way, Moses stands with his finger pointed toward the heavens.
[24] The outstretched hand of Fair Catch Corby, located in the center of

campus in front of the Golden Dome, appears to be signaling for a fair catch.

[25] *See* Daniel L. Wann & Nyla R. Branscombe, *Die-Hard and Fair Weather Fans: Effects of Identification and BIRGing and CORFing Tendencies*. 14 JOURNAL OF SPORT AND SOCIAL ISSUES (1990). The BIRG phenomena will appear occasionally in this book. CORF refers to Cutting-off Reflected Failure and is more attributable to fair-weather fans.

[26] Neither do my London-based university press publishers (Oxford and Cambridge). I have also taught at Loyola University Chicago and George Washington University, but neither has fielded a football team for decades. And while my first teaching assignment, Monmouth College (Illinois), does have a (pretty decent, generally) team, it is a D-III.

[27] Grantland Rice, NEW YORK HERALD-TRIBUNE (October 18,1924).

[28] JOE GARNER, ECHOES OF NOTRE DAME FOOTBALL (2001).

[29] *Id.*

[30] Issac Lorton, *Respect Fuels Navy-Notre Dame Rivalry*, THE OBSERVER (October 21, 2014) at http://ndsmcobserver.com/2014/10/lorton-respect-fuels-navy-notre-dame-rivalry-oct-31/

[31] *Id.*

[32] *Id.*

[33] http://www.navysports.com/ot/ask-the-ad-footbl-scheduling.html

[34] BARRY WILNER & AND KEN RAPPAPORT, GRIDIRON GLORY, THE STORY OF THE ARMY-NAVY FOOTBALL RIVALRY 10 (2005).

[35] Kevin Van Valkenburg, *Army-Navy Rivalry Often a Family Affair*, BALTIMORE SUN 1D (Dec. 2, 2007).

[36] *Id.*

[37] Mike Klingaman, *Clash Provides Break From War; Rivalry Returns to City, First Time Since 9/11; Military Showdown*, BALTIMORE SUN 1A (Dec. 1, 2007).

[38] *Id.*

[39] *Id.*

[40] Gary Lambrecht, *A Blow to the Heart; College Football: The death of one of its own in Iraq jars Navy with extra force*, BALTIMORE SUN 1C (Dec. 2, 2004).

[41] *Id.*

[42] Chet Gordon, *Why Army Football Matters*, TIMES HERALD-RECORD ONLINE (Nov. 30, 2007), accessed at http://www.recordonline.com/apps/pbcs.dll/article?AID=/20071130/SPORTS/711300365/-1/SPORTS01.

[43] Archie Griffin, at https://www.youtube.com/user/OhioStateBuckeyescom

[44] Liz Robbins, *Clisters Wins on Penalty Assessed Against Williams*, NEW YORK TIMES (Sept. 12, 2009), accessed at http://www.nytimes.com/2009/09/13/sports/tennis/13women.html
[45] Massachusetts State Collegiate Athletic Conference, *Framington State Women's Soccer Honored by NCAA* (May 26, 2008), accessed at **http://www.mascac.com/news/07-08news/FramNCAAaward.**
[46] http://www.kansascity.com/105/story/1452971.html
[47] Daniel Brown, *A Timeout to salute a moment of sportsmanship* (May 14, 2009) accessed at http://blogs.mercurynews.com/49ers/2009/05/14/a-timeout-to-salute-a-moment-of-sportsmanship/
[48] Don Lechman, Notre Dame vs USC: The Rivalry 14-15 (2012).
[49] *Id.* at 13.
[50] *Id.*, at 76.
[51] PHELPS, *supra* note 19, at 183.
[52] PHELPS, *supra* note 19, at 183.
[53] LECHMAN, *supra* note 48.
[54] *Id.* at 65.
[55] *Id.* at 125.
[56] College Swimming (Sept. 20, 2009), accessed at **http://collegeswimming.com/news/2009/sep/10/swimmer-wins-ncaa-sportsmanship-award/**
[57] Jamie Maloney observed a West Chester swimmer upset because her goggles broke just one heat before her scheduled race. Maloney did not hesitate to give her own goggles to the swimmer, even it could have cost her school the team championship. Maloney said, "I hope someone would do the same for me." PSAC Swimming, Clarion's Maloney Honored as Division II Sportsmanship Winner (Oct. 29, 2009) accessed at (**http://www.psacsports.org/news/2009/10/29/WSWIM_1029095 019.aspx.**
[58] Kyle Brinzda, *Why I'm Thankful* (Nov. 27, 2014), accessed at http://irish.nbcsports.com/2014/11/27/notre-dame-football-players-why-im-thankful/.
[59] PHELPS, *supra* note 19, at 61-62.
[60] PHELPS, *supra* note 19, at 64.
[61] PAUL WEISS, THE PHILOSOPHY OF SPORT at 14.
[62] Dr. Hans Watson, *Want National Respect? Follow Notre Dame's fans' example,* (May 18, 2015), accessed at http://www.deseretnews.com/article/865628761/Guest-commentary-Want-national-respect-Follow-Notre-Dames-example.html?pg=all
[63] V. Dalakas, R. Madrigal, & D.F. Anderson. *"We are number one!": The phenomenon of basking-in-reflected-glory and its implications for sports marketing* in SPORTS MARKETING AND THE PSYCHOLOGY

OF MARKETING COMMUNICATION 67 (L. R. Kahle & C. Riley ,eds. 2004).
[64] As Robert Madrigal explains, Basking in reflected glory refers to an individual's inclination to "share in the glory of a successful other with whom they are in some way associated" Central to the BIRG effect is one's desire to increase an association with a successful other, such as a sports team, even though the connection is relatively trivial or seemingly incidental." Robert Madrigal, *Cognitive and Affective Determinants of Fan Satisfaction with Sporting Event Attendance* 27 JOURNAL OF LEISURE RESEARCH 205, 207 (1995).
[65] WEISS, *supra* note 61, at 152.
[66] WANN, *supra* note 1, at 377.
[67] Merrill J. Melnick, *Searching for Sociability in the Stands: A Theory of Sports Spectating* 7 JOURNAL OF SPORTS MANAGEMENT 744 (1993).
[68] Smith, G.J., Patterson, B., Williams, T., & Nogg, J. (1981). *A profile of the deeply committed male sports fan,* 5 ARENA REVIEW 26 (1981).
[69] *Id.*
[70] Jim Elliott, *Proud to be a Mountaineer* at http://www.wvulonestarchapter.org/2009/10/proud-to-be-a-mountaineer/
[71] *WVU fans classless no more* (Oct. 29, 2009) accessed at http://www.thedaonline.com/sports/wvu-fans-classless-no-more-1.829173
[72] Cohen, Sharon, *Morning of Terror at Va. Tech Campus,* WASH. POST, (APR. 16, 2007), accessed at http://www.washingtonpost.com/wp-dyn/content/article/2007/04/16/AR2007041601545.html.
[73] Schulte, Brigid and Tim Craig, *Unknown to Va. Tech, Cho Had a Disorder*, WASH. POST, (Aug. 27, 2007) at A01.
[74] Heidi Potter, Heidi's Blog: Sportsmanship (Nov. 26, 2014), accessed at http://www.wlky.com/entertainment/heidis-blog-sportsmanship/29940822
[75] http://www.wndu.com/home/headlines/Tim-McCarthy-has-delivered-his-final-season-of-safety-messages-at-Notre-Dame-Stadium-299861631.html
[76] http://www.wndu.com/home/headlines/Tim-McCarthy-has-delivered-his-final-season-of-safety-messages-at-Notre-Dame-Stadium-299861631.html
[77] Adam Wollner, *Facing Media Blitz Obama Leans on Football Metaphors* (Nov. 14,2013), accessed at http://www.npr.org/sections/itsallpolitics/2013/11/14/245249980/facing-media-blitz-obama-leans-on-football-metaphors
[78] *Id.*

[79] *Id.*
[80] *Id.*
[81] Governor Ted Strickland, *Address to the 2008 Democratic DNC Convention* (August 26, 2008), accessed at http://www.clevelandleader.com/node/6568
[82] Governor Sarah Palin, Resignation Speech, (July 3, 2009), accessed at http://www.huffingtonpost.com/2009/07/03/sarah-palin-resignation-s_n_225557.html
[83] David G. Savage, *Roberts Sees Roles as Judicial "Umpire"*(September 13, 2005), accessed at http://articles.latimes.com/2005/sep/13/nation/na-roberts13.
[84] LOU CANNON, PRESIDENT REAGAN: THE ROLE OF A LIFETIME (1991).
[85] Words of Notre Dame. Notre Dame Magazine. www.adthis.com/bookmark/php?v=250
[86] http://www.brainyquote.com/
[87] Words of Notre Dame. Notre Dame Magazine. www.adthis.com/bookmark/php?v=250
[88] http://www.idiomconnection.com/sports.html
[89] If these are not enough, here are some more from a Wikipedia entry:

>Come out fighting or come out swinging
>Down and out
>Down for the count
>Down to the wire
>Drop the ball
>Drop the gloves
>End run
>Full-court press
>Gambit
>Get the ball rolling
>Glass jaw
>The gloves are off
>Got the distance
>Go to the mat
>Move the goalposts
>Hands down
>Hail Mary
>Hat-trick
>Have someone in your corner
>Heavy hitter
>Heavyweight
>Hit below the belt
>Home stretch

Hospital pass
Hurler on the ditch
Infighting
KO
Keep one's eye on the ball
Keep the ball rolling
Kisser
Knock for six
Knockout
Lead with one's chin
Lightweight
Low blow
Monday morning quarterback
No holds barred
By a nose
On the ropes
One-two punch
Out for the count
Out of the park
Par for the course
Play ball
Pull one's punches
Punch-drunk
Punchy
Push it over the goal line
Quarterback
Ringer
Ringside judge
Ringside seat
Roll with the punches
Round
Run interference
Saved by the bell
Sideline
Slam dunk
Slap-happy
Sparring partner
Square off
Sticky wicket
Stumped
Sucker punch
Sunday punch
Take a dive
Take it on the chin
Take off the gloves

Take the full count
Throw in the towel
Throw one's hat into the ring
Thursday morning tippy tapps
Under the wire
Win by a nose
Wheelhouse
Work out

[90] https://www.nd.edu/fighting-for/2014/fighting-to-design-a-better-home/
[91] One wonders what the reaction would be had this nickname been hung on the Fighting Irish today. With (very legitimate in my view) controversies over mascot names like the Washington Redskins, would a name meant as a negative moniker take hold as it has over a hundred years? *See, e.g.*, Dennis J. Banks, TRIBAL NAMES AND MASCOTS IN SPORTS 1993.
[92] *See,* JOHN KRYK, NATURAL ENEMIES: THE NOTRE DAME-MICHIGAN FOOTBALL FEUD (1994).
[93] *Id.*
[94] Notre Dame Fun Facts: Q&A, accessed at http://www.funtrivia.com/en/Sports/Notre-Dame-Fighting-Irish-4121.html.
[95] Senator Sam Brownback, *The Real Clear Politics Blog, The Brownback Interview*, http://realclearpolitics.blogs.time.com/2007/03/12/the-brownback-interview/# (March 12, 2007).
[96] Derek DeCloet, *Wilson panel skates around reciprocity*, THE GLOBE AND MAIL (Canada) (June 28, 2008).
[97] Ben McGrath, *Nails Never Fails; Baseball's most improbable post-career success story*, THE NEW YORKER, (March 24, 2008).
[98] *See* Bob Katz, *Stop Thinking Business in Like competitive Sports*, FORBES MAGAZINE ONLINE (Jul. 7, 2010).
[99] LOU HOLTZ, WINS, LOSSES AND LESSONS (2006).
[100] LOU HOLTZ, FIGHTING SPIRIT: A CHAMPIONSHIP SEASON AT NOTRE DAME (1989)
[101] HOLTZ, *supra* note 100.
[102] FRANLIN FOER, HOW SOCCER EXPLAINS THE WORLD: AN UNLIKELY THEORY OF GLOBALIZATION (2006)
[103] Melnick, *supra* note 67.
[104] FOER, *supra* note 103, at 49.
[105] FOER, *supra* note 111, at 4.
[106] WEISS, *supra* note 61, at 3
[107] WEISS, *supra* note 61, at 14.

[108] WEISS, *supra* note 61, at 9.
[109] WEISS, *supra* note 61, at 152.
[110] WEISS, *supra* note 61, at 177
[111] CHRISTOPHER H. EVANS & WILLIAM R. HERZOG II, THE FAITH OF FIFTY MILLION 2 (2002).
[112] COOPER, *supra* note 16, at 130.
[113] COOPER, *supra* note 16, at 129.
[114] Ben Kercheval, http://collegefootballtalk.nbcsports.com/2013/01/10/one-bcs-computer-still-has-notre-dame-ranked-no-1/
[115] **Men's (7)**
Cross Country (1): 1957
Fencing (3): 1977, 1978, 1986
Golf (1): 1944
Soccer (1): 2013
Tennis (1): 1959
Women's (5)
Basketball (1): 2001
Fencing (1): 1987
Soccer (3): 1995, 2004, 2010
Co-ed (4)
Fencing (4): 1994, 2003, 2005, 2011
- ACC national team championships
- List of NCAA schools with the most NCAA Division I championships

Below are the 3 National team titles that are not recognized by the NCAA:
- Men's:
  - Basketball (2): 1927, 1936

Tennis (1): 1944
http://www.nd.edu/about/facts/
[116] http://www.nd.edu/about/facts/
[117] See, e.g. Times Higher Education Rankings at https://www.timeshighereducation.com/world-university-rankings/2016/world-ranking#!/page/0/length/25/sort_by/rank_label/sort_order/asc/cols/rank_only
[118] *See,* Bloomberg Businessweek rankings, accessed at http://www.bloomberg.com/features/2016-best-undergrad-business-schools/.
[119] Facts and Figures about Notre Dame at http://www.nd.edu/about/facts/
[120] Ecclesiastes 3 (King James Version).
[121] J.J. Stanwiecz, Why American Pharoah's Triple Crown is Good news for Notre Dame (June 7, 2015) at

[122] http://www.csnchicago.com/notre-dame/why-american-pharoahs-triple-crown-good-news-notre-dame

[123] For a scathing indictment of Notre Dame:

"Television is the Pandora's Box of college sports. Whatever problems we had before television have multiplied in the electronic wasteland. Let us take just one school, our most famous in the world of football, which is exceptional but also representative of aspirations of other "powers." Because of television, Notre Dame is now in the national goldfish bowl with no way out. Its involvement in the world of entertainment only deepens. First, there were the bowls, then membership in the College Football Association, with its complicated television packaging. Then in 1990 Notre Dame arranged its own private package for televising its games, including the annual lopsided one with Navy, as if both schools were still living in the High Roman period. (Even Father Hesburgh has started pulling for Navy, at least for Navy to score, In memory of the good old days no doubt). For the right to televise Notre Dame's home games through 1995, the National Broadcasting Company agreed to pay the University around $375 million. In making this deal, Notre Dame reneged on its promises to be part of the College Football Association made three weeks earlier (Jaeger and Looney 276). One must not feel sorry for the CFA, however. On the Prudential College Scoreboard for September 18, 19832 Jim Lamply reported that at a meeting of presidents to discuss the new CFA alignment not a word was said about academics or the education of the athlete. The only subject, he said, was money. Now another lucrative possibility looms on the horizon, The NCAA football playoff, which will come as sure as the sunrise…One Saturday in the fall of 1988 at half time of a Notre Dame game, a member of the Notre Dame Board of Trustees, also the chairman of the board of Coca Cola, came on television to remind us that Knute Rockne had been a chemist and that synthetic rubber had been discovered in the laboratories of Notre Dame. These seemingly innocent remarks contain much that is wrong with college football. First there is the implication that when we watch college football we should break out the periodic table instead of Budweiser. Second, there is the more than subtle faint suggestion that Rockne is also the father of science at Notre Dame, maybe even responsible for synthetic rubber. Third, there is the indication that the current arrangement between power football and academics issue and healthy, not only at Notre Dame but everywhere, since it meets with the approval of the lords of Coca Cola. Here is the familiar patronization by the athletic business complex of arts and sciences."
ROBERT J. HIGGS, GOD IN THE STADIUM: SPORTS AND RELIGION IN

AMERICA 223-224 (1995).

[124] It is worth bearing in mind that one reason college sports can command such allegiances is because they aren't going anywhere. Professional franchises do, on occasion, relocate, messing with fan loyalty. But one doesn't really have to worry about Notre Dame, Texas, or Michigan going anywhere and so one can go "all-in". For a study on the impact of relocation of sports fan bases see Michael Lewis, *Franchise Relocation and Fan Allegiance*, 25 JOURNAL OF SPORT & SOCIAL ISSUES 6 (2001).

[125] It's a little difficult even to know where one would start with the topic since so many people have said so many things about the topic for so many years. However, as a starting point, one might look at ANTONY FLEW THERE IS A GOD (2007). Flew's account is interesting because of his history. As a youth, he was the son of a minster, but as an adult (and scholar) he became a leading atheist critic of the belief in God. He debated many theistic scholars including some with Notre Dame faculty affiliations, namely Alvin Plantinga and Ralph McInerry. Late in life, however, Flew changed his mind that there is a God. His history does provide him with an interesting perspective with which to introduce a reader to the leading arguments for and against the existence of God in a relatively concise way. For those with a more literary bent, I have always been drawn to Fyodor Dostoyevksy's The Brothers Karamazov, the film version of which I show to my classes each term to conclude the course. Of course, others will have their favorite philosophers, theologians, and writers, but if I had to recommend where to start, I'd start with Flew and Dostoyevsky.

[126] Michael NOVAK, The Joy of Sports (1976).

[127] *Id.* at xii.

[128] *Id.* at xii.

[129] CHRISTOPHER H. EVANS & WILLIAM R. HERZOG II, THE FAITH OF FIFTY MILLION 4 (2002).

www.ingramcontent.com/pod-product-compliance
Lightning Source LLC
Chambersburg PA
CBHW070808100426
42742CB00012B/2288